COLD-CASE
CHRISTIANITY
PARTICIPANT'S GUIDE

A HOMICIDE DETECTIVE INVESTIGATES
THE CLAIMS OF THE GOSPELS

COLD-CASE
CHRISTIANITY
PARTICIPANT'S GUIDE

A HOMICIDE DETECTIVE INVESTIGATES
THE CLAIMS OF THE GOSPELS

J. WARNER
WALLACE

DAVID C COOK

transforming lives together

COLD-CASE CHRISTIANITY PARTICIPANT'S GUIDE
Published by David C Cook
4050 Lee Vance Drive
Colorado Springs, CO 80918 U.S.A.

Integrity Music Limited, a Division of David C Cook
Brighton, East Sussex BN1 2RE, England

The graphic circle C logo is a registered trademark of David C Cook.

The website addresses recommended throughout this book are offered as a resource
to you. These websites are not intended in any way to be or imply an endorsement
on the part of David C Cook, nor do we vouch for their content.

Unless otherwise noted, all Scripture quotations are taken from the New American Standard Bible®,
copyright © 1960, 1995 by The Lockman Foundation. Used by permission. (www.Lockman.org.)
Scripture quotations marked ESV are taken from the ESV® Bible (The Holy Bible, English Standard
Version®), copyright © 2001 by Crossway, a publishing ministry of Good News Publishers. Used by
permission. All rights reserved. The author has added italics to Scripture quotations for emphasis.

ISBN 978-1-4347-1144-1
eISBN 978-0-8307-7549-1

© 2018 James Warner Wallace
Published in association with the literary agency of Mark Sweeney & Associates, Bonita Springs, FL 34135.

Illustrations by J. Warner Wallace
The Team: Stephanie Bennett, Amy Konyndyk, Jack Campbell, Susan Murdock
Cover Design: Nick Lee
Cover Photo: Shutterstock

Printed in the United States of America

First Edition 2018

2 3 4 5 6 7 8 9 10 11

071318

CONTENTS

DON'T BE A "KNOW-IT-ALL" AND LEARN HOW TO "INFER"

I was thirty-five years old before I first paid attention to a pastor's sermon. A fellow officer had been inviting me to church for many months, and while I was able to put him off for some time, I eventually acquiesced and attended a Sunday-morning service with my family. I managed to ignore most of what the pastor talked about until he began to paint a picture of Jesus that caught my attention. He characterized Jesus as a really smart guy who had some remarkably wise things to say about life, family, relationships, and work. I began to believe that this might be true. While I was uninterested in bowing my knee to Jesus as God, I was at least willing to listen to Jesus as a teacher. A week later I purchased my first Bible.

Something about the Gospels caught my attention, more as an investigator than as someone interested in the ancient philosophy of an imaginary sage. By this time in my life, I had already served as a patrol officer and a member of the Gang Detail, the Metro Team (investigating street narcotics), the SWAT Team, and the Crime Impact Team (investigating career criminals). I had interviewed hundreds (if not thousands) of eyewitnesses and suspects. I had become familiar with the nature of eyewitness statements, and I understood how testimony was evaluated in a court of law. Something about the Gospels struck me as more than mythological storytelling. The Gospels actually appeared to be ancient eyewitness accounts. I began carefully employing my investigative training in Forensic Statement Analysis (FSA) to the gospel of Mark. Within a month, and in spite of my deep skepticism and hesitation, I concluded that Mark's gospel was the eyewitness account of the apostle Peter.

In my current assignment, I investigate cold-case murders. Unlike other lesser crimes, an unsolved homicide is never closed; time doesn't run out on a murder investigation.

There are many similarities between investigating cold cases and investigating the claims of Christianity. Cold-case homicides are events from the distant past for which there is often little or no forensic evidence. These kinds of cases are sometimes solved on the basis of eyewitness testimony, even though many years have passed between the point of the crime and the point of the investigation.

Christianity makes a claim about an event from the distant past for which there is little or no forensic evidence. Like cold cases, the truth about what happened can be discovered by examining the statements of eyewitnesses and comparing them with what additional evidence is accessible to us. If the eyewitnesses can be evaluated (and their statements can be verified by what we have available), an equally strong circumstantial case can be made for the claims of the New Testament. But, are there any reliable eyewitness statements in existence to corroborate in the first place? This became the most important question I had to answer in my personal investigation of Christianity. Were the gospel narratives eyewitness accounts or were they only moralistic mythologies? Were the Gospels reliable or were they filled with untrustworthy, supernatural absurdities? The most important questions I could ask about Christianity just so happened to fall within my area of expertise.

I hope to share some of that expertise with you in this study. A quote from C. S. Lewis in his book *God in the Dock* has stuck with me through the years. Lewis correctly noted, "Christianity is a statement which, if false, is of no importance, and, if true, is of infinite importance. The one thing it cannot be is moderately important." Christianity, if true, is worthy of our investigation.

OPEN THE CASE FILE
(5 MINUTES – CONSIDER AND ANSWER AS MANY QUESTIONS AS POSSIBLE)

1.   How would you define the word "faith"?

_____

_____

_____

Some people define faith as believing in something even when there isn't any evidence for it. What role do you think evidence ought to play in our Christian faith?

_____

_____

_____

 Think about how you became a Christian. What role, if any, did evidence play in your decision to become a Christian?

_____

_____

_____

 What would you say to someone who said they didn't think there was any evidence for Christianity?

_____

_____

_____

 VIEW THE VIDEO TESTIMONY
(10 MINUTES – TAKE NOTES)

Controlling your presuppositions (trying not to be a "know-it-all")

_____

_____

Letting the evidence speak for itself when it comes to Christianity

_____

_____

Understanding the difference between "possible" and "reasonable"

_____

_____

Employing "Abductive Reasoning"

_____

_____

Evaluating the alternative explanations for the resurrection

_____

_____

 **CONDUCT A GROUP INVESTIGATION**
(23 MINUTES – INVESTIGATE THE ISSUES AND ANSWER THE QUESTIONS)

Christians are often accused of being "biased" simply because we believe in the supernatural. This accusation has power in our current pluralistic culture. Biased people are seen as prejudicial and unfair, arrogant and overly confident of their position. Nobody wants to be identified as someone who is biased or opinionated. But make no mistake about it, all of us have a point of view; all of us hold opinions and ideas that color the way we see the world. Anyone who tells you they are completely objective and devoid of presuppositions has another more important problem: he (or she) is either astonishingly naïve or a liar.

The question is not whether or not we have ideas, opinions, or preexisting points of view; the question is whether or not we will allow these perspectives to prevent us from examining the evidence objectively. It's possible to have a prior opinion, yet leave this presupposition at the door in order to examine the evidence fairly. We ask jurors to do this all the time. In the state of California, jurors are repeatedly instructed to "keep an open mind throughout the trial" and not to "let bias, sympathy, prejudice or public opinion influence your decision." The courts assume that people have biases, hold sympathies and prejudices, and are aware of public opinion. In spite of this, jurors are required to "keep an open mind."

 In the following diagram from *Cold-Case Christianity*, fill in three presuppositions people might possess in a jury trial. Then fill in three presuppositions people might have when considering the claims of Christianity:

PHILOSOPHICAL NATURALISM

The presuppositional belief that only natural laws and forces (as opposed to supernatural forces) operate in the world. Philosophical naturalists believe that nothing exists beyond the natural realm.

Dangerous Presuppositions for Jurors

Dangerous Presuppositions for Truth Seekers

 People often develop presuppositions from watching the Christians in their lives. In general, how might we live as Christians to prevent our friends and family members from developing presuppositional biases against Christianity?

_____

_____

_____

 There are times when our friends or family members resist our efforts to share the truth about Christianity. How might the understanding of the "beyond a reasonable doubt" standard of proof help us overcome their resistance?

_____

_____

_____

Imagine you have been called to the scene of a DBR (a "Dead Body Report"), as J. Warner described in the video. Use abductive reasoning to determine the most reasonable explanation. Examine the scene illustrated below (from the book *Cold-Case Christianity*). Given the evidence described in the diagram, which of the four potential explanations is most reasonable? Cross out the explanations that are unreasonable, then write why you think the explanation you've picked is most reasonable:

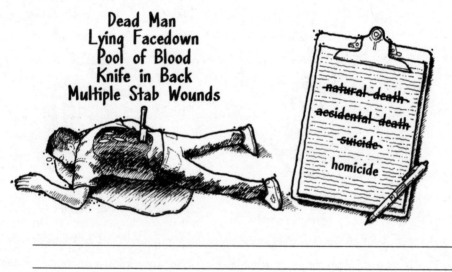

Dead Man
Lying Facedown
Pool of Blood
Knife in Back
Multiple Stab Wounds

~~natural death~~
~~accidental death~~
~~suicide~~
homicide

_____

_____

_____

 Abductive reasoning is a skill each of us can employ on a daily basis. Pick one of the following activities and describe how abductive reasoning might be used to make the best decision:

     1. Purchasing a new car.

     2. Deciding who to marry.

     3. Deciding what is true about God.

_____

_____

_____

Dr. Gary Habermas has taken the time to identify the "minimal facts" (or evidences) related to the resurrection. While there are many claims in the New Testament related to this important event, not all are accepted by skeptics and wary investigators. Dr. Habermas surveyed the most respected and well-established historical scholars and identified a number of facts that *are* accepted by the vast majority of researchers in the field.

Consider the following minimal facts about the resurrection:

1. Jesus died on the cross and was buried.

2. Jesus's tomb was empty and no one ever produced His body.

3. Jesus's disciples believed that they saw Jesus resurrected from the dead.

4. Jesus's disciples were transformed following their alleged resurrection observations.

In the diagram below, four explanations have been offered to explain these simple facts. Begin the process of abductive reasoning by working as a group to write the strengths and weaknesses of each explanation (refer to *Cold-Case Christianity* chapter 2 for assistance completing the diagram). Note that the first three explanations could be offered by someone who *rejects* the truthfulness of the resurrection or the claims of Christianity. The fourth explanation is, of course, the *Christian* explanation:

THE MINIMAL-FACTS APPROACH

Gary Habermas (Distinguished Research Professor at Liberty Baptist Theological Seminary) has popularized the "minimal-facts" approach to examining the resurrection. He limited his list of facts to those that were strongly supported (using the criteria of textual critics) and to those facts that were granted by virtually all scholars (from skeptics to believers). Habermas eventually wrote about his findings in *The Case for the Resurrection of Jesus*.

Explanation	Strengths	Weaknesses
Jesus didn't really die on the cross		
The disciples lied about the Resurrection		
The disciples hallucinated the Resurrection		
The Resurrection truly occurred		

 Now, given the evidence you've examined in the chart and the evidence described in the following diagram, which of the four potential explanations is most reasonable? Cross out the explanations that are unreasonable, then write why you think the explanation you've picked is most reasonable:

Jesus Died and Was Buried
The Tomb Was Empty
The Disciples Claimed to See Jesus Resurrected
The Disciples Were Transformed

Jesus didn't die
The disciples lied
They hallucinated

The Resurrection occurred as they reported it

_____

_____

_____

TAKE A PERSONAL ASSESSMENT
(5 MINUTES OR MORE – EXAMINE YOUR OWN SITUATION AND ANSWER THE QUESTIONS)

Think back to before you were a Christian. What presuppositional beliefs or interests do you think you might have held that distracted or prevented you from hearing the claims of Christianity? How did you overcome them?

_____

_____

_____

_____

_____

Do you think you have enough evidence (beyond your own personal experience) to demonstrate to others that God exists or that Christianity is true? What kind of evidence would you share?

_____

_____

_____

FORM A STRATEGIC PLAN
(5 MINUTES – EXAMINE YOUR CALENDAR AND CREATE AN ACTION PLAN)

Think about the presuppositions of one person you would like to see come to faith, and write them down in the space provided. What might you do specifically to help them recognize that we all hold presuppositions?

_____

_____

_____

Good intentions alone rarely take us very far in our efforts. Are you willing to make a strategic plan of action and commit your plan to a date on a calendar? If so, write down a date this week, _____, when you will initiate a plan of action to begin addressing the presuppositions of the person(s) you identified above.

MAKE A CLOSING STATEMENT
(1 MINUTE – CONTEMPLATE AND PRAY)

Like other nonbelievers in our world today, I used to think of *faith* as the opposite of *reason*. In this characterization of the dichotomy, I believed that atheists were reasonable "free-thinkers" while believers were simple, mindless drones who blindly followed the unreasonable teaching of their leadership. But if you think about it, *faith* is actually the opposite of *unbelief*, not *reason*. As I began to read through the Bible as a skeptic, I came to understand that the biblical definition of faith is a well-placed and reasonable inference based on evidence. I wasn't raised in the Christian culture and I think I have an unusually high amount of respect for evidence. Perhaps this is why this definition of faith comes easily to me. I now understand that it's possible for reasonable people to examine the evidence and conclude that Christianity is *true*. While my skeptical friends may not agree on how the evidence related to the resurrection should be interpreted, I want them to understand that I've arrived at my conclusions reasonably.

Dear God, we thank You for Your many generous gifts. We pray that we will return Your gift of love by loving You in return with all our heart, soul, and mind. Help us to use our minds as we reason with others about the truth of Christianity. Let us be aware of presuppositions and engage others with tools of reason You provide. We want to share Your truth and Your love with everyone. In Jesus's name we pray, amen.

CONDUCT A SECONDARY INVESTIGATION
(READ ON YOUR OWN FOR BETTER UNDERSTANDING)

To better understand the issues raised in this session, read the alternative explanations for the resurrection of Jesus listed in *Cold-Case Christianity* chapter 2: "Learn How to 'Infer.'" Take notes specifically for the section entitled "An Ancient Death-Scene Investigation" (pages 40–50).

_____

_____

_____

_____

_____

_____

_____

_____

_____

_____

THINK "CIRCUMSTANTIALLY" AND TEST YOUR WITNESSES

"Mr. Strickland, how can you be so sure that this man is the same man who robbed you?" The defendant's attorney stood up as he examined the witness and pointed to the man sitting next to him at the defense table. His questions were becoming more accusatory. "Isn't it true that the robbery occurred well after sunset?"

"Well, yes, it was about 10:30 at night." Mr. Strickland seemed to be preparing himself for an attack. He correctly interpreted the tone of the attorney's question and straightened himself in the witness box. He scratched his arm nervously. I knew that Mr. Strickland was a smart guy and I was curious to see how he would hold up under this pressure. I had been working the Robbery/Homicide desk when I was assigned this case, and I knew it would all come down to Mr. Strickland's identification of the suspect.

"I notice you are wearing glasses today, but isn't it true that you weren't wearing those glasses on the night of the robbery?" The defense attorney began to walk slowly toward Mr. Strickland, his arms crossed, his chin slightly elevated as he glanced briefly at the jury.

"I had my glasses on to start with, but I got punched and they flew off my head," replied Mr. Strickland as he pushed his glasses up on his nose. "After that I'm not sure what happened to them." Mr. Strickland's testimony started off calmly enough under the direct questioning of the Deputy District Attorney, but now he seemed to be losing his confidence under the pressure of the cross-examination.

"How long did this episode with your attacker last?" the defense attorney asked.

"Just a few seconds," replied Strickland.

"So let me get this right. You're willing to send my client to jail for years, yet you only saw the suspect for a few seconds, late at night, in the dark, without the benefit of your glasses?" The defendant's attorney was now facing the jury. His question was rhetorical; he made his point and was now watching the jury to see if it had the impact he intended.

"Well, I-I'm not sure what to say," Mr. Strickland stammered hesitantly as he sank in his chair.

The prosecutor was an energetic, competent attorney who understood the value of this victim's eyewitness testimony. She waited for the defense attorney to return to his seat and then prepared for her re-direct. "Mr. Strickland, you said earlier that you were robbed by this man. I want to ask you a question. Given your observations of the robber prior to the moment when he punched you; your observations of the suspect's height, the shape and features of his face, his body-type and the structure of his physique, I want you to rate your certainty about the identity of the suspect. On a scale of 1 to 100, how certain are you that this man sitting here at the defendant's table is the man who robbed you?"

Mr. Strickland sat up in his chair and leaned forward. He paused just slightly before answering. "I am 100 percent certain that this is the man who robbed me. There is no doubt in my mind."

The jury returned a verdict in less than thirty minutes and convicted the defendant, largely on the strength of Mr. Strickland's eyewitness testimony. While the defense attorney did his best to illustrate the potential limits of the victim's ability to accurately describe the suspect, the jury was convinced that Mr. Strickland was a competent eyewitness. Many of my cold cases have hinged on eyewitness testimony. But how can we be certain a witness is telling the truth or has offered an accurate description? Learning how to investigate circumstantial evidence and evaluate eyewitnesses is critical to solving criminal cases. It's also critical to determining whether Christianity is true.

OPEN THE CASE FILE

(4 MINUTES - CONSIDER AND ANSWER AS MANY QUESTIONS AS POSSIBLE)

Think about recent news reports you've heard involving criminal cases. In any of these reports, was the term "circumstantial evidence" referenced? Do your best to define it:

_____

_____

 What do you think most people mean when they use this term? Is circumstantial evidence considered in a positive or negative way? Why?

_____

_____

_____

Have you ever caught someone lying? How did you eventually discover the lie?

_____

_____

 Imagine someone you know made a claim about another friend. How might you attempt to determine if this claim was true or reliable?

_____

_____

_____

VIEW THE VIDEO TESTIMONY
(13 MINUTES – TAKE NOTES)

Understanding the evidential categories and the nature of "circumstantial evidence"

_____

_____

_____

Building a direct-evidence case

An Eyewitness is 100% Certain She Can Identify the Suspect

_____

_____

_____

Building a circumstantial-evidence case

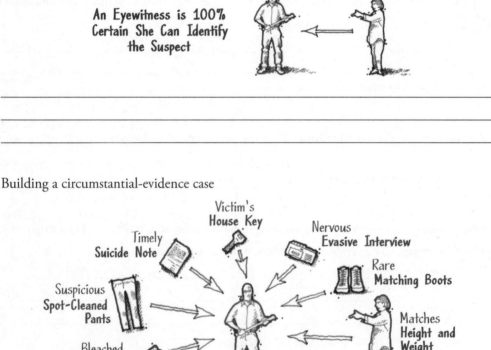

_____

_____

_____

Comparing direct and circumstantial evidence

_____

_____

_____

Testing your eyewitnesses

Present?

_____

_____

Corroborated?

_____

_____

Accurate over Time?

_____

_____

Biased?

_____

_____

Investigating any differences we may find in the gospel accounts

_____

_____

_____

JURY INSTRUCTIONS RELATED TO WITNESSES

1. How well could the witness see, hear, or otherwise perceive the things about which the witness testified?

2. How well was the witness able to remember and describe what happened?

3. What was the witness's behavior while testifying?

4. Did the witness understand the questions and answer them directly?

5. Was the witness's testimony influenced by a factor such as bias or prejudice, a personal relationship with someone involved in the case, or a personal interest in how the case is decided?

6. What was the witness's attitude about the case or about testifying?

7. Did the witness make a statement in the past that is consistent or inconsistent with his or her testimony?

8. How reasonable is the testimony when you consider all the other evidence in the case?

9. Did other evidence prove or disprove any fact about which the witness testified?

10. Did the witness admit to being untruthful?

11. What is the witness's character for truthfulness?

12. Has the witness been convicted of a felony?

13. Has the witness engaged in [other] conduct that reflects on his or her believability?

14. Was the witness promised immunity or leniency in exchange for his or her testimony?

CONDUCT A GROUP INVESTIGATION
(23 MINUTES – INVESTIGATE THE ISSUES AND ANSWER THE QUESTIONS)

Jurors are instructed to make *no* qualitative distinction between direct and circumstantial evidence in a case. Judges tell jurors, "Both direct and circumstantial evidence are acceptable types of evidence to prove or disprove the elements of a charge, including intent and mental state and acts necessary to a conviction, and neither is necessarily more reliable than the other. Neither is entitled to any greater weight than the other." Jesus also understood the importance of both forms of evidence when making a case for His identity. Divide your group into three smaller sets and examine one of the following verses from the gospel of John as you try to identify whether the evidence Jesus is offering is direct or indirect (circumstantial). When you're done, come back together and share your findings.

Read John 10:22–25. To what evidence did Jesus point His followers? Was this evidence direct or indirect?

_____

_____

_____

Read John 5:31–37. In this passage, Jesus cited both forms of evidence. Focus first on John 5:31–35. To what evidence did Jesus first point His listeners? Was this evidence direct or indirect?

_____

_____

_____

Now focus on John 5:36–37. To what additional evidence did Jesus then point His listeners? Was this evidence direct or indirect?

_____

_____

_____

 Read John 10:31–33. To what evidence did Jesus point His detractors? Was this evidence direct or indirect?

_____

_____

Jurors have a duty to take an unbiased look at witnesses and assume the best in them until they have a reason to do otherwise. Jurors are told to "set aside any bias or prejudice [they] may have, including any based on the witness's gender, race, religion, or national origin." In addition, jurors are instructed: "If the evidence establishes that a witness's character for truthfulness has not been discussed among the people who know him or her, you may conclude from the lack of discussion that the witness's character for truthfulness is good" (Section 105, Judicial Council of California Criminal Jury Instructions, 2006). We should also apply this principle to the biblical eyewitnesses. Return to your three smaller groups and examine one of the following verses to answer the following questions. When you're done, come back together and share your findings.

 Read 1 Peter 5:1 and 2 Peter 1:16–17. What role did Peter see himself playing as a disciple of Jesus and apostle? What specific words did he use to make this clear?

_____

_____

_____

 Read John 21:24 and 1 John 1:1–3. What role did John see himself playing as a disciple of Jesus and apostle? What specific words did he use to make this clear?

_____

_____

_____

 Read Luke 1:1–4. Luke was not an eyewitness to the life and ministry of Jesus. What role did Luke see himself playing as an author? What specific words did he use to make this clear?

_____

_____

_____

Why is it appropriate for us to ask good investigative questions related to eyewitness reliability ("Were they present?"; "Can they be corroborated?"; "Did they change their story over time?"; and "Were they biased?") when evaluating the authors of the Gospels?

_____

_____

_____

_____

_____

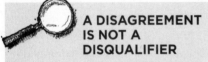

A DISAGREEMENT IS NOT A DISQUALIFIER

Jurors are instructed to be cautious, not to automatically disqualify a witness just because some part of his or her statement may disagree with an additional piece of evidence or testimony: "Do not automatically reject testimony just because of inconsistencies or conflicts. Consider whether the differences are important or not. People sometimes honestly forget things or make mistakes about what they remember. Also, two people may witness the same event yet see or hear it differently." (Section 105, Judicial Council of California Criminal Jury Instructions, 2006)

Many years ago, I investigated a robbery in which a male suspect entered a small market, walked up to the counter and calmly contacted the cashier. The suspect removed a handgun from his waistband and placed it on the counter. He pointed it at the cashier, using his right hand to hold the gun on the counter, his finger on the trigger. The suspect quietly told the cashier to empty the register of its money and place it in a plastic bag. The cashier complied and gave the robber all the money in the drawer. The robber then calmly walked from the store. This robbery was observed by two witnesses (Sylvia and Paul) who were properly separated and interviewed apart from one another. Now look at the following diagram to see the differences in their accounts:

Sylvia Ramos
- 38-yr-old Female
- Married with Kids
- Interior Designer
- Picking Up Milk on the Way Home from Work

Paul Meher
- 23-yr-old Male
- Single, No Kids
- Apprentice Plumber
- Visiting the Cashier on His Day Off

How They Described the Suspect

Younger Boy in His Teens	Man About 24-25 Years Old
Very Polite with Sweet Voice	Threatening Scowl
Did Not Have a Gun	Had a Ruger P95 9mm Handgun
Bought Something at the Store	Bought Nothing at the Store
Wore an Izod Polo Shirt	Might Have Worn a T-Shirt
Had No Vehicle	Ran to a 90s Tan Nissan

Why do you think these details varied between the two witnesses? List what might be true about their personal histories, interests, and location within the business that might account for the differences:

_____

_____

_____

TAKE A PERSONAL ASSESSMENT
(4 MINUTES – EXAMINE YOUR OWN SITUATION AND ANSWER THE QUESTIONS)

Where have seemingly different Bible passages caused you to doubt in the past? Can you see now how these passages might be explained? If you don't have a personal example, read the parallel accounts of the Lord's Supper found in the gospels of Matthew (Matt. 26:17–30) and John (John 13:1–14:7). Write down some of the differences between these two eyewitness accounts:

Matthew:

John:

_____ _____
_____ _____
_____ _____
_____ _____
_____ _____
_____ _____
_____ _____

Now, imagine you are explaining to a skeptic why these apparent contradictions do not make the Bible unreliable. What would you say?

_____
_____
_____

FORM A STRATEGIC PLAN
(5 MINUTES – EXAMINE YOUR CALENDAR AND CREATE AN ACTION PLAN)

Set aside time this week (schedule it on your calendar) to scan (or reread if you have time) the synoptic gospels (Matthew, Mark, and Luke) and select three parallel events that exist in each gospel (i.e. the baptism of Jesus, the healing of the paralytic, or the feeding of five thousand). Given what you now know about how a witness's personal interests, history, and geographic location impact how he or she describes an event, how do apparent differences affect your level of confidence in the accounts?

_____

_____

_____

 Choose someone you know who would benefit from what you've learned about eyewitness testimony: _____

 Select a parallel event from the Gospels to share with this friend: _____

_____

 Set a date and time when you plan on sharing: _____

MAKE A CLOSING STATEMENT
(1 MINUTE – CONTEMPLATE AND PRAY)

The gospel eyewitnesses observed uniquely powerful and memorable events and provided us with accounts that are distinctive, idiosyncratic, personal, and reliable. We simply need to take the time to understand the perspective and character of each eyewitness and then determine if the accounts are trustworthy given the four criteria we have described. Given the strength of the eyewitness testimony and circumstantial evidence we find in Scripture, we can be confident as we share the good news of the gospel with others.

 Dear Lord, You are sovereign over all. We humbly thank You for the evidence You have given us as You have awakened our interest through Your Holy Spirit. Your Son, Jesus Christ, provided us with evidence through the miracles He performed in front of the eyewitnesses who testified about Him. They stood by their testimony even under severe persecution and threat of

THE CHOSEN APP

death. Help us to recognize the reliability of Your Word and be able to convey Your truth to others. We ask this in the name of Jesus, amen.

CONDUCT A SECONDARY INVESTIGATION
(READ ON YOUR OWN FOR BETTER UNDERSTANDING)

To better understand the issues raised in this session, read *Cold-Case Christianity* chapters 3 and 4. Take specific notes related to the reasons why eyewitnesses sometimes report an event differently (see pages 80–81):

Eyewitness Statements Will Be Perspectival:

_____

_____

_____

Eyewitness Statements Will Be Personal:

_____

_____

_____

Eyewitness Statements May Contain Areas of Complete Agreement:

_____

_____

_____

Later Eyewitness Statements May Fill in the Gaps:

_____

_____

_____

HANG ON EVERY WORD AND SEPARATE ARTIFACTS FROM EVIDENCE

After an exhausting day of interviews, we were really no closer to having a suspect in view. We were still looking for a trailhead, a direction that would lead us to the suspect who killed a young woman in our city in 1981. We managed to locate all the men and women who had been suspected of this crime many years ago and arranged interviews with them. Eight hours into these meetings, I was still undecided about who might be the most likely candidate for the murder. Then Scott Taylor said something that caught my attention.

Scott dated the victim about one year prior to the murder. He had been interviewed back in 1981, along with many other men who dated or knew her. The original investigators had been unable to single out any one of these men as a primary suspect. Today, Scott said something that seemed unusual. It wasn't anything big. In fact, my partner didn't catch it at all.

We asked each candidate how he or she "felt" about the victim's murder. We were careful to ask the question the same way each time we asked it; the responses were important to us as we tried to understand the relationships between the potential suspects and the victim. One responded, "I'm shocked that someone could have killed her." Another told us, "It's tragic, I hope you guys catch the killer." A third said, "Although we had problems, I was devastated when I learned about it." Scott said something very different.

"Let me ask you, Scott, how did you feel about her death? Did you have any feelings about it one way or the other?" I asked him casually, hoping to gauge his response.

Scott paused for a second, choosing his words. He shrugged his shoulders slightly and said, "Well, I was sorry to see her dead, you know. We didn't always get along but it's never good to see anyone die."

Of all the possible responses that Scott could have offered, this one struck me as odd and a bit telling. It may have simply been a figure of speech that was common to Scott—I would have to interview him more thoroughly to see if I could provoke a similar response about something else—but it was interesting that Scott's first reply to our question was that he was "sorry to see her dead." We knew the killer stood over the victim's body and made sure she was dead by nudging her. It could reasonably be said that the killer "saw her dead" prior to leaving the scene. Was Scott inadvertently telling us something about his involvement in this crime?

It would be another year before we would complete our investigation. Ultimately, we learned a lot more about Scott's relationship with the victim and we eventually determined that he killed her because he didn't want anyone else to date her following their breakup. We discovered a large amount of circumstantial evidence that came together to make our case. Scott's statement about "seeing her dead" pointed us in his direction and was eventually used in court (along with everything else we learned) to convict him. Was this statement enough, on its own, to make our case? Of course not. But, it was consistent with Scott's involvement and truly reflected the way he felt in the moments following the murder.

Scott's case taught me the value of paying close attention to every word a suspect might offer. We all choose the words we use. Sometimes we choose as a matter of habit. Sometimes we choose words that reflect, either consciously or subconsciously, the truth about how we feel or the truth about what really happened. I've learned to hang on every word. In this session, we'll apply this principle and approach to the Gospels.

OPEN THE CASE FILE
(4 MINUTES – CONSIDER AND ANSWER AS MANY QUESTIONS AS POSSIBLE)

We often miss the importance of words because, as readers, we skip over them too lightly, or, as listeners, we are more concerned about what we plan on saying in response than we are in paying attention to what is being said. Good detectives (and good investigators of the Gospels) must learn how to pay attention to word choices.

Rate yourself as a listener on a scale from 1 to 10. If you consider yourself a good listener, describe why you think that is the case. If you don't consider yourself a good listener, identify two or three reasons why that might be the case: My Rating as a Listener: _____

_____

_____

_____

In your opinion, what makes a good listener? List three or four attributes of people who listen well.

_____

_____

_____

VIEW THE VIDEO TESTIMONY
(13 MINUTES – TAKE NOTES)

Hanging on every word

_____

_____

_____

Thinking about the nature of Forensic Statement Analysis

_____

_____

_____

Examining the gospel of Mark

TRANSCRIPT OF TEACHINGS OF PETER

_____

_____

Investigating the claims of skeptics like Bart Ehrman

_____

_____

_____

Using the principles of Crime Scene Investigation to study the differences between the ancient manuscripts of the Gospels

_____

_____

_____

Comparing copies to discover and correct the differences in manuscripts

_____

_____

_____

CONDUCT A GROUP INVESTIGATION
(23 MINUTES – INVESTIGATE THE ISSUES AND ANSWER THE QUESTIONS)

When I first started investigating the Gospels, a Christian friend told me that Mark's gospel was really the eyewitness account of the apostle Peter. The early church seemed to agree. Papias (AD 60–130), the ancient Bishop of Hierapolis (located in Western Turkey), claimed that Mark penned his gospel in Rome as Peter's scribe. He reported that "Mark, having become the interpreter of Peter, wrote down accurately, though not in order, whatsoever he remembered of the things said or done by Christ." Other early church leaders and students of the apostles (from diverse geographic regions) also repeatedly and uniformly claimed that Mark's gospel was a record of Peter's eyewitness observations.

As I began to study Mark's gospel forensically, I observed a number of interesting anomalies related to Peter. These peculiarities seemed reasonable if Peter was, in fact, Mark's source for information. Divide your group into fourths, read the following passages of Scripture, and answer the questions:

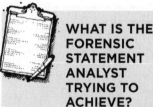

WHAT IS THE FORENSIC STATEMENT ANALYST TRYING TO ACHIEVE?

Forensic Statement Analysts carefully examine the words offered by witnesses and suspects in an effort to determine:

1. Is the writer (or speaker) more involved in the event than they might like us to believe?

2. Are there relational problems between the writer (or speaker) and the victim who is the subject of the case?

3. What are the hidden difficulties between the writer (or speaker) and the victim in the investigation?

4. Was the writer (or speaker) actually doing what they claimed to be doing at the time of the crime?

5. Should the writer (or speaker) be considered as a suspect in this crime under consideration?

Read Mark 1:16 and 16:7. Now read the passage preceding Mark 1:16 and following Mark 16:7. Are any disciples mentioned other than Peter? Why would Mark begin and end his gospel in this way? Why might this be important in identifying the source of Mark's information as he wrote this account?

_____

_____

_____

Read Luke 5:1–11 and Mark 1:16–20. Which words and descriptions related to Peter and the miraculous catch of fish are missing from Luke's account? How might Mark's special relationship to Peter explain the differences in these two accounts?

_____

_____

_____

 Read Matthew 21:18–19 with Mark 11:20–21. How does Mark mention Peter uniquely in his account? Why might Mark mention Peter in a way that Matthew did not?

_____

_____

_____

 Read Acts 1:21–22 and 10:37–41. Notice how Peter, when talking about Jesus, omits details of Jesus's private life and limits his descriptions to Jesus's public ministry, death, resurrection, and ascension. How is this similar to the rough outline of Mark's gospel? How might this explain Peter's unique relationship to Mark?

_____

_____

_____

Now reunite as a group and examine the following diagram (from *Cold-Case Christianity*, p. 94). Seven lines of evidence (described in this section

REASONS WHY SCRIBES SOMETIMES CHANGED THE TEXT

It's clear that scribes occasionally changed the biblical manuscripts when copying them. The vast majority of these changes were completely unintentional (simple misspellings or grammatical errors). Some, however, were intentional:

1. Some intentional alterations were performed in an effort to harmonize passages that describe the same event in two separate gospels (parallel passages).

2. Some intentional alterations were done to add detail known to the scribe, but not clearly described by the apostolic author.

3. Some intentional alterations were made to clarify a passage of Scripture based on what a scribe thought the passage meant (the scribes were not always correct in their interpretation).

and in the video) have been illustrated in this cumulative case for Peter's influence in Mark's gospel. Work together to insert the applicable verse examples into four of the seven lines of evidence:

Skeptic Bart Ehrman, as described in the video, draws attention to variations between ancient manuscripts of the Gospels. It's true that scribes who copied the Scripture sometimes made a mistake or added something to the text, but this doesn't mean that we can't reliably redact these small, inconsequential variations and return to the inerrant Word of God. Gather again in your four smaller groups and pick one of the following passages to investigate variations made to the ancient manuscripts:

 Read Luke 22:39–44. Verses 43 and 44 do not appear in early manuscripts of Luke's gospel:

> "And there appeared an angel unto him from heaven, strengthening him. And being in an agony he prayed more earnestly: and his sweat was as it were great drops of blood falling down to the ground" (KJV).

They have been omitted from some modern Bible translations (like the RSV). While the KJV does not isolate them as late additions, other translations (like the

NIV, NASB, and NKJV) identify them as such in footnotes or special brackets. Why might these verses have been inserted by a scribe? Why doesn't their insertion affect anything we might know about the nature of Jesus or the doctrines of Christianity?

_____

_____

_____

Read John 5:1–4. The last few words of verse 3 and all of verse 4 don't appear in the best ancient manuscripts:

> "For an angel went down at a certain season into the pool, and troubled the water: whosoever then first after the troubling of the water stepped in was made whole of whatsoever disease he had" (KJV).

Several modern translations have simply removed the verse (i.e., the NIV, RSV, and NRSV) while others have identified it in the footnotes (i.e., the NKJV and ESV). Why might these verses have been inserted by a scribe? Why doesn't their insertion affect anything we might know about the nature of Jesus or the doctrines of Christianity?

_____

_____

_____

Read 1 John 5:1–7. The second half of verse 7 does not appear in any manuscript of the Bible until the sixteenth century (and it only appears in two manuscripts at this point in history):

> "… the Father, the Word, and the Holy Ghost: and these three are one." (KJV)

It has been omitted from modern translations like the NASB and NIV and identified with a footnote in the NKJV. Why might these verses have been inserted by a scribe? Why doesn't their insertion affect anything we might know about the nature of Jesus or the doctrines of Christianity?

_____

_____

_____

 Read Acts 15:30–35. The earliest and most reliable manuscripts do not contain verse 34:

"Notwithstanding it pleased Silas to abide there still." (KJV)

Modern translations like the NIV, RSV, and NRSV have removed it, while the NASB, NKJV, and ESV have identified it with brackets or a footnote. Why might these verses have been inserted by a scribe? Why doesn't their insertion affect anything we might know about the nature of Jesus or the doctrines of Christianity?

_____

_____

_____

Reunite as a large group. None of these additions or variants have any impact on what we know about Jesus or the broad orthodox claims of Christianity, and although they may exist in some ancient manuscripts, we can identify them and remove them to return reliably to the inerrant original versions of the Gospels. Let me show you how this is done.

Imagine that you are my patrol partner one afternoon as we are working beat 514C. We get a call from dispatch on our MDT (the mobile computer in our police unit) that summons us to a robbery that is taking place at a local mini-mart. The dispatch operator sends us the call but accidentally types the wrong street name and misspells the weapon. We recognize that there is no street by this name in our city, but we are aware of the fact that a very similar street (with the same hundred block) does exist in our beat. As we head in that direction, we notify dispatch and receive a new communiqué with the corrected street name. In this second dispatch, however, the operator makes an additional error and misspells the word "Markey." We again notify the dispatcher and receive yet another message, but once again, there is a misspelling. The dispatcher makes two more repeated efforts to correct the misspelling, but in the pressure of the moment (remember a robbery is occurring), she is never quite able to do it without some form of error:

Dispatch: 211 Now	514C:
1426 Crosbit Street, 7-11 Market, WMA, blue-steel handbun	Crosbie Street?
Dispatch: 211 Now	514C:
1426 Crosbie Street, 7-11 Markey, WMA, blue-steel handbun	10-9?
Dispatch: 211 Now	514C:
1426 Crosbie Street, 7-11 Market, WMA, blue-steel handbun	Weapon?
Dispatch: 211 Now	514C:
1428 Crosbit Street, 7-11 Market, WMA, blue-steal handgun	Location?
Dispatch: 211 Now	514C:
1426 Crosbit Street, 7-11 Market, WMA, blue-steal bandgun	10-4

Now let me ask you a question: With the robbery in progress and time of the essence, should we stop at the curb and wait for dispatch to type the call correctly, or do we have enough information, given the growing number of duplicated lines being sent by the dispatcher, to proceed to the call? The more copies of the message we possess, the more we can compare them to determine the dispatcher's original meaning, and the more confidence we can have in our conclusion. Something very similar to this occurs when we examine literally thousands of existing ancient biblical manuscripts. Yes, we can see the variants and late additions, but that's the beauty of our large manuscript collection: it allows us to remove the inaccuracies with confidence.

TAKE A PERSONAL ASSESSMENT
(4 MINUTES – EXAMINE YOUR OWN SITUATION AND ANSWER THE QUESTIONS)

While it is true that we *do not* have an original copy of the Gospels and there are differences between the ancient manuscripts we *do* possess, we have enough manuscripts to compare and return reliably to the inerrant original message of Scripture. We've separated the artifacts from the evidence; we've returned the biblical "crime scene" to its original condition. That being said, most Christians are largely unaware of the fact that we don't possess the biblical "autographs" (original copies), and you might not have been aware of this fact either:

 Did you know, prior to this study, that there were variations between the oldest existing New Testament manuscripts? Imagine hearing this for the first time from a skeptic like Bart Ehrman. How do you think this information would have impacted your confidence in the Bible? Why would it have had this kind of impact on you?

_____

_____

_____

 Take the time here to rehearse how you might respond to the skeptical objection offered by Bart Ehrman, "There are more variations between the ancient manuscripts than there are words in the New Testament." In the following space, craft a response based on what you know about the process of textual analysis you learned in this lesson:

_____

_____

_____

_____

_____

_____

_____

_____

_____

_____

_____

FORM A STRATEGIC PLAN
(5 MINUTES – EXAMINE YOUR CALENDAR AND CREATE AN ACTION PLAN)

As always, what gets calendared gets done. There is likely someone in your life who will be challenged by the skeptical claims we've been studying related to the ancient manuscripts. Now is the time to help those who are still ill-equipped. Take the time right now to identify someone in your life who might need to know how much confidence we can have in the New Testament message. Set a date to talk with them about the manner in which we are able to return to the original message of the Bible:

Identify the person you want to equip: _____

Set a date to share: _____

It's one thing to have confidence that the message of the gospel authors has been delivered to us accurately; it's another to know that message well enough to share it with others. Take action today and set a date to read one of the four gospels from beginning to end (in one setting):

Pick a gospel to read: _____

Set a date to read it in one setting: _____

After reading it, summarize the most memorable and powerful "takeaway" you had from your reading:

_____

_____

_____

MAKE A CLOSING STATEMENT
(1 MINUTE – CONTEMPLATE AND PRAY)

Hebrews 4:12 states, "For the word of God is living and active and sharper than any two-edged sword, and piercing as far as the division of soul and spirit, of both joints and marrow, and able to judge the thoughts and intentions of the heart." God's Word is thorough, precise, and powerful! Every single word He has given us has eternal significance and meaning. Reread this verse, several times, aloud. Let the impact of each and every word of this verse penetrate your heart, soul, and mind.

Dear heavenly Father, You are the author and perfecter of our faith. You tell us in 2 Timothy 3:16–17, "All scripture is God-breathed and is useful for teaching, rebuking, correcting, and training in righteousness, so that the man of God may be thoroughly equipped for every good work." Please fill us with Your knowledge and wisdom as we diligently read Your Word, paying careful attention to each and every word You have given us. In Your precious Son's name we pray, amen.

CONDUCT A SECONDARY INVESTIGATION
(READ ON YOUR OWN FOR BETTER UNDERSTANDING)

The information in this lesson has been taken from *Cold-Case Christianity*, chapter 5: "Hang on Every Word," and chapter 6: "Separate Artifacts from Evidence." Read these two chapters to better understand the concepts. The appearance and nature of variants in the ancient manuscripts can be troubling for many people, so focus on the principles scholars use of removing artifacts from evidence and take good notes on this section (pages 102–4). These techniques are similar to what detectives do when investigating crime scenes:

Identify the Late Additions

_____

_____

_____

_____

Recognize Differences in Character

_____

_____

_____

_____

Look for an Explanation

_____

_____

_____

_____

See What Happens If You Include It

_____

_____

_____

_____

Rely on What You Know

_____

_____

_____

_____

Session Four

RESIST CONSPIRACY THEORIES, KNOW WHEN "ENOUGH IS ENOUGH," AND PREPARE FOR AN ATTACK

"Charlie, your roommate already told us where to find the green plaid shirt you were wearing last night." Charlie sat with his head down and his hands on his thighs. His body language communicated his continuing resistance to my questioning. This last statement, however, caused the first small reaction I had seen all afternoon. Charlie finally lifted his head and looked me in the eyes. "You and I both know I'm gonna find the victim's blood on that shirt." Charlie sat there quietly. I could tell that he believed my lie about his roommate.

Eighteen hours earlier, Charlie and his roommate, Vic, attempted to rob Dennis Watkins as he was walking home from his girlfriend's house. A simple street robbery turned into a homicide when Dennis decided he was bigger than Charlie and struggled with him for his knife. Charlie stabbed Dennis only once, but the resulting chest wound was fatal. The robbery took place late at night in an alley to the rear of a fast-food restaurant in our town. There were no witnesses and no one else was on the street at the time of the robbery, but Charlie was unknowingly recorded by a surveillance camera located on a bank across the alley. While the camera was too far away to identify the killer facially, it did record the unusual green plaid shirt worn by one of the two attackers and captured an image of their general height and build. Several hours later (through a series of investigative efforts), we had Charlie and Vic in custody, but we had little evidence to corroborate their involvement. We needed a "cop-out" if we hoped to file the case with the district attorney.

We separated Charlie and Vic as soon as we arrested them; Vic was in a second interview room down the hall. I had not yet interviewed him; I lied to Charlie about the conversation. Vic didn't tell me where to find the plaid shirt. Charlie just happened to better match the physical build of the primary suspect I saw on the video, so I took a stab at him as the suspect who wore the shirt. I could tell I was right by Charlie's reaction. He was fidgeting in his chair and turned his gaze to the floor again. I stayed silent and let my statement hang in the air. Charlie finally looked up.

SOME POPULAR CONSPIRACY THEORIES

Lee Harvey Oswald didn't act alone when he killed President Kennedy.

The US government was involved in the 9/11 disaster.

The 1969 Apollo moon landing was fabricated.

A UFO crashed in Roswell, New Mexico.

"Vic's lying about that. He's the one who gave me that shirt for my birthday, but he wears it more than I do." Charlie folded his arms again and leaned backwards, trying to increase the distance between the two of us.

That was all I needed, really—just another small piece of information. I left Charlie for a moment and entered the room with Vic. I pulled a chair up to the table that separated us, introduced myself, and got down to business.

"Vic, I just got done talking to Charlie. Murder is a serious crime, and he told me that you were the one who stabbed this guy. He told me about the green plaid shirt. He said that you gave that shirt to him for his birthday, but you wear it more than he does. He told us where to find it. He said we'll find the victim's blood on the shirt and he's willing to testify against you, bud."

Within fifteen minutes, Vic told us all about the crime and confirmed what we had seen on the video. He provided many details about their prior plan to commit the robbery, and he confirmed his secondary involvement in the attack. He also told us that Charlie was the man who stabbed Dennis and he provided us with the location of the knife. It's not easy for two or more people to lie about an event and hold firm in their lie under pressure. Successful conspiracies are far rarer than most people think. In this session, we'll examine the nature of successful conspiracies, learn how much evidence is necessary to make a reasonable inference, and examine the strategies of those who try to deny the truth.

OPEN THE CASE FILE
(5 MINUTES – CONSIDER AND ANSWER AS MANY QUESTIONS AS POSSIBLE)

Skeptics who doubt the truth of Christianity sometimes argue the disciples lied about the resurrection of Jesus. How would you respond to this objection?

_____

_____

_____

What would you say to someone who says there are too many unanswered questions about God or Jesus to be certain enough to know if God exists or Christianity is true?

_____

_____

_____

How would you respond to someone who says they can't believe Christianity is true because they know many Christians who have done harmful things or who are presently engaged in evil behavior?

_____

_____

_____

VIEW THE VIDEO TESTIMONY
(11 MINUTES – TAKE NOTES)

Understanding what's required for a successful conspiracy

_____

_____

_____

_____

_____

_____

Examining the "Standard of Proof"

_____

_____

_____

_____

_____

_____

Preparing for an attack from the "other side"

_____

_____

_____

_____

_____

_____

CONDUCT A GROUP INVESTIGATION

(23 MINUTES – INVESTIGATE THE ISSUES AND ANSWER THE QUESTIONS)

History is filled with examples of men and women who were committed to their religious views and were willing to die a martyr's death for what they believed. The hijackers who flew the planes into the Twin Towers in 2001, for example, considered themselves to be religious martyrs.

 Does the martyrdom of modern-day religious believers testify to the truth of their beliefs in a manner similar to the martyrdom of the twelve apostles? Why or why not?

_____

_____

_____

 Many of us, as Christians, would be willing to die rather than deny Jesus or reject the truth claims of Christianity. But, how is our willingness to die for the truth today different than the willingness of the apostolic eyewitnesses in the first century?

_____

_____

_____

 Why is the death of the apostles a much better evidence for the veracity of Christianity than any modern-day martyrdoms?

_____

_____

_____

There are many reasons why people may deny (or "shun") the truth. Not all reasons are based on evidence. Jurors can reject a truth claim for "ra'shun'al," "emo'shun'al," or "voli'shun'al" reasons (yes, I am abusing the English language in an attempt to make these three reasons memorable). Sometimes jurors have rational doubts that are based on the evidence. Perhaps the defense has convinced them that an alternative explanation is better supported evidentially. Sometimes jurors have doubts that are purely emotional. I've been involved in cases where jurors had an emotional reaction to the prosecutor or defense attorney and struggled to overcome negative feelings so they could evaluate the case fairly. Sometimes jurors deny the truth for volitional reasons. They are willfully resistant and refuse to accept any position offered by the group.

Examine the following statements made by people who reject Christianity and indicate which of these three reasons is most consistent with the statement:

"My dad was a Christian, and he was a real hypocrite."

This is a form of _____ doubt.

"Christianity is full of dos and donts. It's oppressive."

This is a form of _____ doubt.

"I just don't think there's enough manuscript evidence to believe the claims of Christianity."

This is a form of _____ doubt.

Now read the following biblical passages in which someone had doubt. Try to identify what kind of doubt each person had:

Read Matthew 14:25–31. Peter doubted.

This was a form of _____ doubt.

Read Luke 24:33–39. The disciples doubted.

This was a form of _____ doubt.

Read John 20:24–27. Thomas doubted.

This was a form of _____ doubt.

In trials across America, an escalating "Standard of Proof" is used to adjudicate claims, determine truth, and prosecute wrongdoers. The standard of **"Some Credible Evidence"** is the lowest possible standard (it is used in some child protection hearings). This standard simply establishes that there is enough evidence to begin an inquiry, investigation, or trial. The standard of **"Preponderance of the Evidence"** is the next standard of proof (it is used in most civil trials). This standard is established if a proposition is more likely to be true than untrue (i.e., 51 percent more likely to be true). The standard of **"Clear and Convincing Evidence"** is an intermediate standard of proof (used in some civil and criminal proceedings). This standard is met when a proposition is significantly and substantially more likely to be true than untrue. Finally, the standard of **"Beyond a Reasonable Doubt"** is the highest level of proof required by the law (it is usually reserved for criminal trials). This standard is met when there is no plausible reason to believe that a proposition is untrue.

> Given what you now know about the escalating Standards of Proof, which standard do you think would be most applicable when considering the claims of Christianity? Why would this standard be appropriate?

_____

_____

_____

> Some skeptics say Christianity would have to be demonstrated beyond the possibility of a doubt. Can you think of one or two reasons why this standard would be too high?

_____

_____

_____

Don't be surprised when the opposition offers an alternative explanation that differs from the Christian explanation. In the cases I've been a part of over the years, I've noticed patterns and approaches on the part of defense attorneys that are similar to tactics employed by skeptics of Christianity. In *Cold-Case Christianity* (p. 152), I describe eight tactics employed by those who oppose the truth:

For the sake of brevity, I want to focus on three of these tactics:

Challenge the Nature of Truth. What if all truth was simply a matter of opinion? How might this affect our efforts to communicate the claims of Christianity? Why must we make the case for the existence of objective, transcendent truth claims?

_____

_____

_____

"AD HOMINEM" ATTACKS

"Ad hominem" (Latin for "to the man") is an abbreviated form of "Argumentum ad hominem." It describes what is normally seen as a logical fallacy—the attempt to discredit the truth of a claim by pointing out some negative characteristic, behavior, or belief of the person who is making the claim. Dictionary.com describes "ad hominem" as "attacking an opponent's character rather than answering his argument."

Demand Evidential Perfection. Skeptics often argue that the case for Christianity is imperfect, in that they find it lacking in some way. Given what you now know about the Standard of Proof, how might you help a skeptic overcome the need to answer every possible doubt?

_____

_____

_____

Employ a Culturally Winsome Attitude. Skeptics often employ humor or charm to make their case against Christianity. Why is this approach so powerful? What can we learn from this as we seek to make the case for truth?

_____

_____

_____

 ## TAKE A PERSONAL ASSESSMENT
(5 MINUTES – EXAMINE YOUR OWN SITUATION AND ANSWER THE QUESTIONS)

Have you ever thought about how a jury is required to come to a decision, even without being able to obtain an answer to every question they had during the trial? How have you handled your own questions related to God, the Bible, or Christianity? List one or two open questions you would still like to have answered:

_____

_____

_____

 Given that the Standard of Proof is "beyond a reasonable doubt" and not "beyond a possible doubt," how will you deal with your unanswered questions?

_____

_____

_____

 All unanswered questions must be evaluated in light of the questions you can answer. Think about the strength of the circumstantial case for Christianity. Make a list of some of the reasons you have for knowing Christianity is true:

_____

_____

FORM A STRATEGIC PLAN

(5 MINUTES – EXAMINE YOUR CALENDAR AND CREATE AN ACTION PLAN)

All inquiries and examinations of the truth (including historical investigations) have their unique deficiencies. Jurors understand they must work with what they have in front of them. You have at your disposal multiple pieces of evidence for Christianity. Choose one area of evidence that you are interested in learning more about and study it this week. Start gathering evidence for a claim about Jesus that you would like to be able to defend. Make a list, write out your discoveries, and consider recording yourself answering a related question. You may even want to orally present your case to someone. Use whichever modality of communication best suits your learning style.

Pick an area you would like to study:

_____

Select potential resources you might use (include books and websites):

_____

_____

Make a brief list of evidences you discover in your study:

_____

_____

_____

_____

_____

_____

MAKE A CLOSING STATEMENT
(1 MINUTE – CONTEMPLATE AND PRAY)

While we are often willing to spend time reading the Bible, praying, or participating in church programs and services (all important activities), few Christians recognize the need to become good Christian *case makers*. We can use the model of a courtroom to master the facts of the case and anticipate the questions we may be asked by friends, family, skeptics, and especially our own children. When we devote ourselves to this rational preparation and study, we are worshipping God with our mind, the very thing He has called us to do (Matt. 22:37).

Dear God, we praise You for Your patience with us as we struggle with our doubts and unanswered questions. Thank You for Your continual grace in providing us with scenarios in our world from which we can draw analogies to understanding the Standard of Proof and reasonable doubt. Give us peace in recognizing the impossibility and unreasonable expectation that every question has to be answered for us to put our trust in You. Fill us with a passion to worship You with all of our heart, soul, and mind. Give us the desire to love our neighbor as our self by learning how to communicate and defend Your Word. In Jesus's name we pray, amen.

CONDUCT A SECONDARY INVESTIGATION
(READ ON YOUR OWN FOR BETTER UNDERSTANDING)

In this session, we've covered material from *Cold-Case Christianity*, chapters 8, 9, and 10. We only briefly discussed the tactics employed by defense attorneys (and skeptics) from chapter 10, so be sure to read and take notes from this section (pages 141–53). The more you know about these strategies, the better prepared you will be to defend the truth of Christianity:

Defense Attorneys Challenge the Nature of Truth

_____

_____

_____

Defense Attorneys Focus on the Best the Prosecution Has to Offer

_____

_____

_____

Defense Attorneys Target the Micro and Distract from the Macro

_____

_____

_____

Defense Attorneys Attack the Messenger

_____

_____

_____

Defense Attorneys Want Perfection

_____

_____

_____

Defense Attorneys Provide Alternative "Possibilities"

_____

_____

_____

Defense Attorneys Employ a Culturally Winsome Attitude

_____

_____

_____

WERE THEY PRESENT?

When I was a nonbeliever, I eagerly accepted the claims of skeptics who denied the reliability of the New Testament. In fact, I often made statements similar to this one made by Bart Ehrman, the New Testament scholar, professor of religious studies, and author of *Jesus Interrupted*:

> "Why was the tomb supposedly empty? I say 'supposedly' because, frankly,
> I don't know that it was. Our very first reference to Jesus's tomb being
> empty is in the Gospel of Mark, written forty years later by someone living
> in a different country who had heard it was empty. How would he know?" ·
> (page 171)

I often argued with Christian friends and coworkers at the police department. Like many skeptics, I was inclined to reject the Gospels as late works of *fiction*. I considered them to be mythological accounts written well after all the true eyewitnesses were dead.

I worked in our Gang Detail and investigated a variety of gang-related assaults. One of them involved a stabbing between members of two rival gangs; both parties were armed with knives. It was hard to determine which of the two gang members was actually the victim, as both were pretty seriously injured and no eyewitnesses were willing to come forward to testify about what really happened. About a year after the case was assigned to me, I got a telephone call from a young lady who told me that she witnessed the entire crime and was willing to tell me how it occurred. She said that she had been deployed as a member of the army for the past year, and, for this reason, she had been unaware that the case was still unresolved. After a little digging, I discovered that this "eyewitness" was actually a cousin of one of the gang members. After a lengthy interview with her, she finally admitted that she was training in another state at the time of the stabbing. She didn't even hear about it until about a week before she contacted me. She was lying to try to implicate the member of the rival gang and protect her cousin. Clearly, her story was a late piece of fiction, created long after the original event for the express purpose of achieving her goal. She wasn't even available or present at the crime to begin with, and for this reason, she was worthless to me as a witness.

As a skeptic, I believed that the Gospels were penned in the second century and were similarly worthless. If they were written that late, they were not eyewitness accounts. It's really as simple as that; true eyewitnesses to the life of Jesus would have lived (and written) in the *first century*. The first criterion of eyewitness reliability requires us to answer the question: "Were the alleged eyewitnesses present in the first place?" Like the unbelieving scholars, I answered this question by arguing that the Gospels were written in the second or third century, far too late to have been written by true eyewitnesses. In the first four sessions of our study, we've examined a number of detective skills. Now we're going to start using these skills to investigate the reliability of the New Testament. We'll begin by investigating the dating of the Gospels to see if they were written early enough to have been written by eyewitnesses.

OPEN THE CASE FILE
(5 MINUTES – CONSIDER AND ANSWER AS MANY QUESTIONS AS POSSIBLE)

How much do you know about your personal family history? Do you know anything about the lives of your grandparents? Write down one fact you know about the childhood of your grandparents:

_____

_____

 Did you learn this fact from your grandparents, or did your parents tell you about this aspect of your grandparents' lives? Why should you trust the accuracy of what your grandparents said about their childhood over what your parents might have told you about your grandparents' lives?

_____

_____

_____

VIEW THE VIDEO TESTIMONY
(9 MINUTES - TAKE NOTES AND FILL IN THE DIAGRAM)

Remembering the four criteria for determining eyewitness reliability

_____

_____

Understanding the importance of early dating

_____

_____

Re-creating the gospel authorship timeline (for help completing the timeline, refer to *Cold-Case Christianity* page 170)

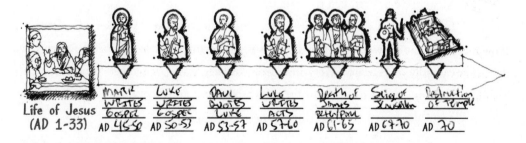

Life of Jesus (AD 1-33)

MARK WRITES GOSPEL — AD 45-50

LUKE WRITES GOSPEL — AD 50-53

PAUL QUOTES LUKE — AD 53-57

LUKE WRITES ACTS — AD 57-60

Death of James, Peter & Paul — AD 61-65

Siege of Jerusalem — AD 67-70

Destruction of Temple — AD 70

Investigating Clues from Paul

1 Timothy 5:17–18

The elders who direct the affairs of the church well are worthy of double honor, especially those whose work is preaching and teaching. For the Scripture says, "Do not muzzle the ox while it is treading out the grain," and "The worker deserves his wages."

_____

_____

_____

1 Corinthians 11:23–25

For I received from the Lord that which I also delivered to you, that the Lord Jesus in the night in which He was betrayed took bread; and when He had given thanks, He broke it and said, "This is My body, which is for you; do this in remembrance of Me." In the same way He took the cup also after supper, saying, "This cup is the new covenant in My blood."

_____

_____

_____

Investigating a Clue from Luke

Luke 1:1–4

Many have undertaken to draw up an account of the things that have been fulfilled among us, just as they were handed down to us by those who from the first were eyewitnesses and servants of the word. Therefore, since I myself have carefully investigated everything from the beginning, it seemed good also to me to write an (orderly) account for you, most excellent Theophilus, so that you may know the certainty of the things you have been taught.

_____

_____

_____

CONDUCT A GROUP INVESTIGATION

(25 MINUTES – INVESTIGATE THE ISSUES AND ANSWER THE QUESTIONS)

Take another look at the timeline. There are many pieces of circumstantial evidence that form a compelling case for the *early* dating of the Gospels. There are several good reasons to believe that the gospel writers are standing on the *left side* of the timeline, very near the events recorded in the Gospels. The more I examined this evidence, the more I came to believe that the Gospels were written early enough in history to be taken seriously as eyewitness accounts. Let's examine some of the scriptural evidence that confirms the early dating of the Gospels:

1. **Have someone in the group read aloud Deuteronomy 25:4.** Have another member of the group locate and read Luke 10:7 (preferably from the NASB version of the Bible). Now compare them to 1 Timothy 5:17–18 (as cited in the video) and circle where Paul quotes these verses in his letter to Timothy. Why do you think Paul cited a New Testament verse to Timothy when the Old Testament verse from Deuteronomy would have been sufficient to make his point?

_____

_____

_____

2. **Have someone in the group read aloud Luke 22:19–20.** Now compare this to 1 Corinthians 11:23–26 and circle the part of the passage in 1 Corinthians where Paul quotes from Luke. Paul planted this church in Corinth a few years before writing this letter, dated from AD 53–57. What does this tell us about the dating of the Luke gospel?

_____

_____

_____

How long do you think Luke's gospel would have existed to be considered so authoritative by this early Christian group?

_____

_____

_____

Have someone in the group read aloud Luke 1:1–4 (preferably from the NASB version of the Bible). Unlike Matthew and John, Luke doesn't appear to be writing his gospel as an eyewitness. How would you identify his role as an author (based on his own description of his efforts)?

_____

_____

_____

To whom is Luke writing his gospel? Who does he say he is interviewing to gather the information for his gospel?

_____

_____

_____

How does this help us to understand why there are so many passages in Luke's gospel that appear to be quoted or paraphrased from the gospels of Matthew and Mark?

_____

_____

_____

WHO IS "THEOPHILUS"?

Many have tried to identify "Theophilus." While no one knows the answer for sure, there are many reasonable possibilities:

He's Every "Friend of God." Some have observed that the word "Theophilus" is Greek for "Friend of God." For this reason, they propose that Luke wrote his works for all those who were friends of God and interested in the claims of Jesus.

He's a Roman Official. Since Luke only uses the expression "Most Excellent" when addressing Roman officials, many believe that Theophilus must have held some similar Roman position.

He's a Jewish High Priest. Others have identified a pair of Jewish High Priests who lived in the first century (Theophilus ben Ananus or Mattathias ben Theophilus), arguing that Luke's focus on the Temple and Jewish customs related to the Sadducees could best be explained if one of these two priests were his intended audience.

While some modern critics challenge the authorship of Paul's Pastoral Letters, even the most skeptical scholars agree that Paul is the author of the letters written to the Romans, the Corinthians, and the Galatians. These letters are dated between AD 48 and AD 60. The Letter to the Romans (typically dated at AD 50) reveals something important. Paul begins the letter by proclaiming that Jesus is the resurrected "Son of God." Throughout the letter, Paul accepts the view of Jesus that the gospel eyewitnesses described in their own accounts. Just seventeen years after the resurrection, Jesus is described as Divine. He is God incarnate, just as the gospel eyewitnesses described in their own accounts. In fact, Paul's outline of Jesus's life matches that of the Gospels.

Have someone in the group read aloud 1 Corinthians 15:3–8. Paul says the truth of the resurrection was "delivered" to him. From whom did Paul learn about the resurrection of Jesus?

_____

_____

_____

This passage in 1 Corinthians is considered by many scholars to be perhaps the earliest creed of Christianity. Review the passage again and work as a group to fill in the following creedal data:

1. Jesus died for our _____.
2. Jesus's death was _____ by the Scripture.
3. Jesus was _____.
4. Jesus rose from the dead on the _____ day.
5. Jesus's resurrection was also _____ by the Scripture.
6. Jesus appeared to _____.
7. Jesus appeared to the other _____.

Paul also says that five hundred brethren saw the resurrected Christ at the same time and that most of these people were still alive at the time he wrote the letter. Why would this be a brave (and even risky) claim to make if it wasn't true?

_____

_____

_____

 Have someone in the group **read aloud Galatians 1:15–19**. In his letter to the churches in Galatia (also written in the mid-50s AD) Paul describes the meeting with two men who witnessed the resurrection and delivered this information to him. Who were these two men and how many years after Paul's experience on the road to Damascus did this meeting take place?

_____

_____

 Now read Galatians 2:1. How many years later did Paul return once again to visit with the eyewitnesses so he could submit to them the gospel he had been preaching among the Gentiles? With whom did he meet?

_____

Given the evidence of 1 Corinthians, Galatians, and the book of Acts, we can now reconstruct the early dating of the creedal information found in 1 Corinthians 15 (let's use the date of AD 33 for the resurrection and ascension of Jesus, for the sake of clarity):

AD 33 – Jesus was resurrected from the grave and ascended to heaven.

AD 34–35 – Jesus appeared to Paul while Paul was on the road to Damascus (one to two years after the resurrection and ascension).

AD 37–38 – Paul received the data about the historicity and deity of Jesus from Peter and James while visiting them in Jerusalem (two to three years after his conversion, depending on how you interpret the words "three years later").

AD 48–50 – Paul corroborates the data about the historicity and deity of Jesus with John, Peter, and James in the presence of Barnabas and Timothy (fourteen years after the Damascus Road event or fourteen years after the first meeting with Peter and James in Jerusalem).

AD 51 – Paul first provided data to the Corinthian church about the historicity and deity of Jesus (during this visit to Corinth, he also appeared before Galileo).

AD 55 – Paul writes to the Corinthian church and reminds them of the data he previously provided them about the historicity and deity of Jesus.

The early Christian creed related to the historicity and deity of Jesus in 1 Corinthians 15 is actually a written record of the earliest transmitted data we have about Jesus.

How close to the event was information about the resurrection of Jesus described and proclaimed to others?

_____

How does this additional data support what we established in the Early Dating Timeline?

_____

TAKE A PERSONAL ASSESSMENT
(4 MINUTES – EXAMINE YOUR OWN SITUATION AND ANSWER THE QUESTIONS)

Have you ever had difficulty digesting information that was only presented in one "modality" (for example, in *auditory* or *written* form)? What is your learning style? How do you learn new information best?

_____

_____

What are some ways you can make biblical information more readily understood by others? How can you quickly determine their learning style?

_____

_____

_____

 How does the visual "early dating timeline" help you (or others) process the case for the dating of the Gospels?

_____

_____

 How might you use this visual tool to help others understand how early the Gospels were written?

_____

_____

 **FORM A STRATEGIC PLAN**
(5 MINUTES – EXAMINE YOUR CALENDAR AND CREATE AN ACTION PLAN)

Timelines are useful visual aids for presenting information. Laying facts out in one concise diagram enables the user to see the "big picture" all at once. You may want to take a photo of the timeline presented in this study guide (to use on your phone) or print a copy of the timeline to use when presenting information related to the dating of the Gospels (you could even keep a copy in your Bible). But if you really want to be prepared to share the truth, the best approach may simply be to memorize the timeline and practice drawing it quickly for others:

 Pick a date to perfect your version of the timeline:

_____

Draw it repeatedly until you can produce the timeline on a napkin or scrap of paper quickly. Use this space to practice drawing the timeline:

 Now practice your ability with a friend or family member. Select someone to practice with: _____

 Select a date and time to practice presenting your presentation:

_____

 ## MAKE A CLOSING STATEMENT
(1 MINUTE – CONTEMPLATE AND PRAY)

Juries *test* witnesses. The first test is simple: Was the witness really there to *see* what they said they *saw*? When evaluating the gospel writers, the most reasonable inference from the evidence is an *early* date of authorship. The Gospels were written early enough to have been written by true eyewitnesses, and (just as importantly) they were written early enough to have been "fact checked" by people who actually knew Jesus personally. The Gospels pass the first test.

 Dear Lord, Your love for us is unfailing. We are extremely grateful for the evidence You have given us through the Bible. Thank You for the details You have included in Your Word and the testimonies of the disciples and eyewitnesses to Jesus's life and ministry here on earth. We ask You to open our eyes, hearts, and minds to the truth in Your Word. In Jesus's name we pray, amen.

CONDUCT A SECONDARY INVESTIGATION
(READ ON YOUR OWN FOR BETTER UNDERSTANDING)

To better understand the issues raised in this session, read *Cold-Case Christianity* chapter 11: "Were They Present?" Given what we covered together, focus on the claims of skeptics presented in this chapter (starting at the bottom of page 171 and continuing to page 179). Use this space to take notes:

The Authors of the Gospels Are Anonymous

_____

_____

_____

The Temple Destruction Is Predicted

_____

_____

_____

The Accounts Are Replete with Miraculous Events

_____

_____

_____

There Was a Second-Century Bishop in Antioch Named "Theophilus"

_____

_____

_____

Luke Agreed with Much of What Josephus Reported

_____

_____

_____

For more information about the earliest creed of the church as described in this lesson, read the work of Dr. Gary Habermas, an expert in this area of study, at www.garyhabermas.com.

WERE THEY CORROBORATED?

Christian Scripture is not merely a collection of proverbs or commandments related to moral living, although the New Testament certainly contains these elements. The Bible is a claim about *history*. Like other eyewitness accounts, the Bible tells us that something happened in the past in a particular way, at a particular time, with a particular result. If the accounts are true, they are not merely "legends," even though they may contain miraculous elements that are difficult for skeptics to accept. It's not surprising that those who reject the supernatural would doubt those who claimed to see something miraculous. It's also not surprising that these skeptics would want miraculous claims to be corroborated.

While there are times when an eyewitness is the only piece of evidence I have at my disposal, most of my cases are buttressed by other pieces of evidence that corroborate the eyewitness. I once had a case from 1982 in which a witness (Aimee Thompson) claimed to see a murder suspect (Danny Herrin) standing in the front yard of the victim's house just minutes before the murder took place. At the time of the original investigation, Aimee identified Danny from a "six-pack photo lineup," a series of six photographs of men (complete strangers to Aimee), arranged in two rows in a photo folder. Aimee did not know Danny personally, but she recognized his face in the photo. She remembered that he was wearing a popular "concert" T-shirt with a logo from the musical band Journey, announcing their tour in support of their *Escape* album. In addition to this, she told me that the man she observed stood in a peculiar way, hunched over just slightly as if he had some sort of physical injury. I knew that Danny also had this unusual posture and fit her description. Given this identification, I traveled out to the city where Danny lived for an interview. When I spoke with Danny, he denied that he was anywhere near the victim's house. In fact, he claimed that he wasn't even in the same city as the victim on that particular day. While it would have been nice to find some forensic evidence at the scene that corroborated Aimee's observations, this was unfortunately not the case. The original investigators did, however, find a gas receipt in Danny's car that had been issued from a gas station on the day of the murder, just a quarter mile from the victim's house. In addition to this, I later interviewed Danny's sister; she told me that Danny mentioned stopping by to see the victim on the day of the murder.

Now it's true that the gas receipt and his sister's statement alone would not prove that Danny murdered the victim, but these two additional facts did corroborate Aimee's claims; if nothing else, her assertions were made more reasonable by her observations of Danny's unusual stance and these additional supporting facts. There were two forms of corroboration working here. First, there was corroboration that was internal to Aimee's statement. She described something that was true about the suspect (his stance), and could not have been known by Aimee unless she was actually present as she claimed. In addition to this internal evidence, there was also external evidence that corroborated her claim. The gas receipt and Danny's sister's statement were independent of Aimee, but still supported her assertions. Together, the internal and external evidence agreed with Aimee's primary claims as an eyewitness.

In this session, we are going to investigate internal and external evidences that support, verify, and corroborate the claims of the Gospels.

OPEN THE CASE FILE
(5 MINUTES – CONSIDER AND ANSWER AS MANY QUESTIONS AS POSSIBLE)

Most of us understand, at least intuitively, the power of corroboration. We hear claims all the time, from advertisers, political and religious leaders, and even from friends and family members. Consider the following claims and think about how you might verify each of them to be certain they are true:

Imagine your teenage son tells you he was an hour past curfew because his car ran out of gas. How might you verify such a claim? What kind of corroborative evidence might you ask for?

_____

_____

_____

 Imagine a car manufacturer claims a particular model in the car line gets the best gas mileage of any car in its class. How would you seek to verify this? What resources would you consult?

_____

_____

_____

 Imagine a Mormon missionary claimed that the Book of Mormon describes an accurate history of the North American continent in the centuries preceding and following the life and ministry of Jesus. How might you corroborate the claims of these missionaries? What forms of evidence would you seek to determine if the history described in the Book of Mormon is accurate?

_____

_____

_____

 VIEW THE VIDEO TESTIMONY
(10 MINUTES – TAKE NOTES)

Defining "internal" and "external" corroborative evidence

_____

_____

_____

Thinking about "internal" corroboration of the Gospels

_____

_____

    Unintentional eyewitness support

    _____

    _____

    Names of cities

    _____

    _____

    Names of men and women in the region

    _____

    _____

Considering "external" corroboration of the Gospels

_____

_____

    Archaeology

    _____

    _____

    Ancient non-Christian authors

    _____

    _____

CONDUCT A GROUP INVESTIGATION
(24 MINUTES – INVESTIGATE THE ISSUES AND ANSWER THE QUESTIONS)

Corroboration from the "Inside Out"

Much has been written about the internal evidences that support the reliability of the New Testament authors; scholars have studied the use of language and Greek idioms to try to discover if the writing styles of each author corroborate the New Testament claims related to the authors. Is

John's use of language consistent with that of a first-century fisherman? Is Luke's language consistent with that of a first-century doctor? While these exercises are interesting from a scholarly perspective, they did not pique my investigative curiosity as a detective. Two areas of internal evidence, however, did interest me as someone who has interviewed hundreds of witnesses:

1. The Gospel Writers Provided Unintentional Eyewitness Support

I described one example of this form of internal corroboration in the video (the passage involving the striking of Jesus). Let's look at another similar example of unintentional eyewitness support. Read the following passages as a group and examine how the first account raises a question that is answered by the second:

"HARMONIZATION" OR "INTERPOLATION"?

When two or more eyewitness accounts are considered by an investigator, it's the duty of the detective to "harmonize" the accounts. The details from each account must be assembled without modifying the statements or adding details that are foreign to the observations of the witnesses. In the end, the final "harmony" will provide us with a version of events in which the voices of all the eyewitnesses can be heard clearly and distinctly, even though they may be providing different details. Detectives must avoid "interpolation," the insertion of additional or extraneous material into the eyewitness record.

Have someone read Matthew 4:18–22 (The Calling of Jesus's Disciples). This passage raises a number of important questions. What were these fishermen doing when Jesus walked up? How quickly did they leave what they were doing to follow Him? Why would they leave to follow Jesus so quickly?

_____

_____

Now have someone read Luke 5:1–11. This passage includes details missing from the first account, and these details explain why the disciples left to follow Jesus without any further delay. What miraculous event, involving Simon, occurred after Jesus arrived but prior to the disciples following Him (vv. 3–8)? How might this help explain why the men left everything so quickly to follow Jesus?

_____

_____

_____

2. The Gospel Writers Referenced Names Correctly

The gospel writers are believed to have written from a number of geographic locations. Mark probably wrote from Rome, Matthew may have written from Judea, Luke from either Antioch or Rome, and John from Ephesus. Skeptics have argued that these accounts were not written by people who had firsthand knowledge of the life and ministry of Jesus, but were simply inventions written generations later by people who weren't all that familiar with the locations they were describing. But historian and lexicographer Tal Ilan discovered just the opposite when she examined the biblical use of *names*.

The most popular names found in the Gospels just happen to be the most popular names found in Palestine in the first century. This is even more striking when you compare the ancient popular Palestinian Jewish names with the ancient popular Egyptian Jewish names:

Top Jewish Men's Names in Palestine	Top Jewish Men's Names in Egypt
Simon	Eleazar
Joseph	Sabbataius
Eleazar	Joseph
Judah	Dositheus
Yohanan	Pappus
Joshua	Ptolemaius

 How does this correct use of names serve as corroborative evidence?

_____

_____

 How could a writer know which names to use if they wrote the accounts late in history or out of the region where the people allegedly lived?

_____

_____

Corroboration from the "Outside In"

Ancient observers and writers who were *hostile* to Christianity reluctantly admitted several key facts that corroborate the claims of the Christian eyewitnesses, even though they denied that Jesus was who He claimed to be. As described in the video, have one member of your group read each non-Christian quotation, then work as a group to create a list of attributes related to Jesus:

Read the passage from the Non-Christian:	Write in the information they provide about Jesus:
Thallus (AD 5?–60?): "On the whole world there pressed a most fearful darkness; and the rocks were rent by an earthquake, and many places in Judea and other districts were thrown down. This darkness Thallus, in the third book of his History, calls, as appears to me without reason, an eclipse of the sun." (*Chronography*, 18:1)	
Tacitus (AD 56–120): "Consequently, to get rid of the report, Nero fastened the guilt and inflicted the most exquisite tortures on a class hated for their abominations, called Christians by the populace. Christus, from whom the name had its origin, suffered the extreme penalty during the reign of Tiberius at the hands of one of our procurators, Pontius Pilatus, and a most mischievous superstition, thus checked for the moment, again broke out." (*Annals*, 15:44)	

Continue to read the passage from the Non-Christian:

Continue to write in the information they provide about Jesus:

Mara Bar-Serapion (AD 70–?):

"What advantage did the Jews gain from executing their wise King? It was just after that that their kingdom was abolished ... Nor did the wise King die for good; He lived on in the teaching which He had given." (Letter from Mara Bar-Serapion to His Son)

_____

_____

_____

_____

_____

_____

Phlegon (AD 80–140):

"Now Phlegon, in the thirteenth or fourteenth book, I think, of his Chronicles, not only ascribed to Jesus a knowledge of future events ... but also testified that the result corresponded to His predictions." (Origen, *Against Celsus*, 2:14)

_____

_____

_____

_____

_____

_____

As diagramed in the following illustration from *Cold-Case Christianity* (p. 201), the ancient non-Christian description of Jesus, although incomplete, is remarkably similar to the description offered by the gospel writers. Early, external, non-Christian sources corroborate the testimony of the New Testament authors.

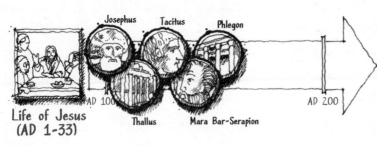

Life of Jesus (AD 1-33)

Josephus · Tacitus · Phlegon · Thallus · Mara Bar-Serapion

AD 100 · AD 200

Lived in Judea
A Virtuous Man
Had Wondrous Power
Could Predict the Future
Was "Wise King" of the Jews
Accused By Jewish Leaders
Crucified by Pilate
During Reign of Tiberius
Darkness and an Earthquake
Reportedly Rose After Death
Believed to Be the Messiah
Called the Christ
Followers Called Christians
A "Superstition" Spread

Because Christianity makes historical claims, archaeology should also be a tool we can use to see if these claims are, in fact, true. Here are just two examples:

 Have someone read John 5:1–9. What pool is described in this passage? Where was this pool located in Jerusalem? How many porticos surrounded the pool?

For many years, there was no evidence for such a place outside of John's gospel; skeptics again pointed to this passage of Scripture and argued that John's gospel was written late in history by someone who was unfamiliar with the features of the city. The twentieth-century discovery of the Dead Sea Scrolls, however, provided us with ancient confirmation of the

THE CORROBORATION OF LANGUAGE

The gospel writers do more than correctly cite the popular names of first-century Palestinian Jews. They also appear to have written in a style that was similar to those who lived at that time. Non-biblical scraps of papyrus and pottery from the first century provide us with samples of the form of Greek that was popular in the ancient Middle East. The Greek used by the gospel writers is very similar to the vernacular "common" Greek that was used by others who lived in this region at this time in history. (Refer to *The New Testament Documents: Are They Reliable?* by F. F. Bruce, 2010.)

pool's existence. In 1888, archaeologists began excavating the area near St. Anne's Church in Jerusalem and discovered the remains of the pool, complete with steps leading down from one side and five shallow porticos on another side.

 Have someone read John 9:1–12, while two other members of the group get ready to read Isaiah 8:6 and 22:9. What pool is described in the gospel of John? For what purpose was the pool used? How is the pool referenced in the passages in Isaiah?

John is the only other ancient author (aside from Isaiah) to ever describe this pool's existence. Scholars were unable to locate the pool with any certainty until its discovery in the City of David region of Jerusalem in 2004. Archaeologists Ronny Reich and Eli Shukrun excavated the pool and dated it from 100 BC to AD 100 (based on the features of the pool and coins found in the plaster). This discovery corroborated the reliability of Christian Scripture and the testimony of John.

There are many other examples of archaeological corroboration listed in *Cold-Case Christianity*.

The Broad Strokes Corroborated by the "External Evidence" of Ancient Non-Biblical Witnesses and Archaeology

The Fine Details Corroborated by the "Internal Evidence" of Names, Locations, Language and "Unintentional Support"

Our picture of Jesus is made clearer by the corroboration of the *internal* evidence as it authenticates the *external* evidence and validates the claims of the gospel writers themselves.

TAKE A PERSONAL ASSESSMENT
(4 MINUTES – EXAMINE YOUR OWN SITUATION AND
ANSWER THE QUESTIONS)

Depending on how you were raised as a Christian, you may or may not appreciate the importance of corroborating your beliefs with evidence. After all, isn't faith supposed to be something we possess *without* any evidence?

1　Describe a time in your life when you experienced doubt about the claims of Christianity:

_____

_____

_____

How might it have helped if you would have known about the evidence that corroborates the claims of Christianity?

_____

_____

_____

2　Do you have any friends or family members who are Mormon, Muslim, Hindu, or Buddhist? These believers, when asked why they believe their worldview is true, will often cite the way they were raised or an experience they might have had. How can corroborative evidence help us determine which of these religious worldviews is actually true?

_____

_____

_____

FORM A STRATEGIC PLAN

(5 MINUTES – EXAMINE YOUR CALENDAR AND CREATE AN ACTION PLAN)

The more we learn about the corroborative evidence for Christianity, the more confidence we ought to have in what we believe as Christians. As a result, we should be excited to share the truth. This week, decide to engage someone you know who holds a different religious worldview. Rather than overwhelm them with evidence for Christianity, simply ask them about their own spiritual journey. Ask them why they are Mormon, Muslim, Hindu, Buddhist, or whatever view they might hold. Then listen carefully and make a note about the nature of their answers:

Someone I know who holds a different worldview: _____

Set a date to listen: _____

Following the conversation, list the reasons they gave for why they thought their view was true:

_____

_____

_____

Now think about how you might be able to share how Christianity is different from other claims about God because it is centered on a historical event (the life, death, and resurrection of Jesus).

Set a date to share: _____

Some of the corroborative evidence you might share:

_____

_____

_____

MAKE A CLOSING STATEMENT
(1 MINUTE – CONTEMPLATE AND PRAY)

In Acts 1:2–3, Luke said that Jesus spent time with the disciples after the resurrection to corroborate His claims: "To these He also presented Himself alive after His suffering, by many convincing proofs, appearing to them over a period of forty days and speaking of the things concerning the kingdom of God." Jesus didn't ask His followers to believe blindly. He understood our desire to verify the claims He made while He was alive. As Christians, we are in the unique position of being able to corroborate our beliefs about God.

Dear Lord, we thank You for Your patience with us. You know that we are prone to skepticism and doubt. Thank You for living among us and providing us with many ways to corroborate Your claims. Thank You for knowing us so well, and honoring our desire to verify what we believe. Now help us to use this greater confidence to grow the kingdom for Your glory. Give us opportunities to share the truth with others, and help us to recall the many ways we can corroborate Your Word for others. In the precious name of Jesus we pray, amen.

CONDUCT A SECONDARY INVESTIGATION
(READ ON YOUR OWN FOR BETTER UNDERSTANDING)

The material in this lesson was excerpted from *Cold-Case Christianity* chapter 12: "Were They Corroborated?" Read through this chapter and take notes:

_____

_____

_____

_____

_____

_____

_____

_____

_____

_____

_____

The following resources are recommended for further study on the topic of corroborative evidence:

> *Hidden in Plain View: Undesigned Coincidences in the Gospels and Acts* by Lydia McGrew (2017): to learn more about the unintentional eyewitness support ("undesigned coincidences") of the New Testament.
>
> *Lexicon of Jewish Names in Late Antiquity: Palestine 330 BCE–200 CE* by Tal Ilan (2002): to learn more about the way the gospel authors used the correct names of men and women in the New Testament.
>
> *The Evidence for Jesus* by R. T. France (2006): to learn more about the non-biblical ancient sources that corroborate the existence of Jesus.
>
> *Archaeology and the New Testament* by John McRay (2008): to learn more about the archaeological corroboration of the New Testament.
>
> *The Final Days of Jesus: The Archaeological Evidence* by Shimon Gibson (2009).

And finally (for fun), you may want to watch *God's Not Dead 2* to see how the Gospels are defended in two courtroom scenes!

WERE THEY ACCURATE?

People who claim that the biblical narratives are mere fiction and filled with error presume that the authors of the Bible operated under the protection of time and distance. False, fictional elements can be inserted into an account if they are inserted well after any living eyewitnesses are alive to identify them as lies. In addition, if the true historical record has not been preserved well, or guarded to prevent corruption, errors can slip in without much notice. If this occurred with the Gospels, they are untrustworthy. Even if they are corroborated at several points by archaeology or internal evidences, they may still be inaccurate about any number of episodes they describe.

Cold-case investigators understand the relationship between time and reliability. We have to evaluate the prior statements of witnesses and suspects and do our best to figure out if these statements are true or fictional. Sometimes the passage of time provides an advantage to cold-case investigators that was not available to the detectives who originally worked the case. Time often exposes the inaccuracy of eyewitnesses and the lies of suspects. I've taken advantage of this over the years.

I once had a case where the suspect (named Jassen) provided an alibi at the time he was originally investigated in 1988. Jassen said that he was driving to a friend's house at the time of the murder, although he never made it there because he had a flat tire. When he said this to the original detectives, they wrote it in their notes. They failed, however, to document Jassen's statement in their final report. They never found enough evidence to arrest Jassen, and as a result, they didn't write an arrest report; their closing reports were far less complete than they would have been if anyone had actually been arrested for this crime.

Years later, I reopened the case and examined the original reports and notes of the first detectives. They had been carefully preserved in our department's Records Division where they were originally copied and stored on microfiche. I saw Jassen's original statement in the first detective's notes and asked this investigator to meet with me. He told me about his interview with Jassen, and without prompting from his notes, he recalled the details of what Jassen said with great accuracy. When I showed him the copy of his notes, he recognized them without hesitation.

I next arranged an impromptu interview with Jassen. While the original detective was careful to take notes about the interview he conducted in 1988, Jassen made no such record. With the passage of time, Jassen forgot what he first told the detective. The story he now gave to me was completely different than the story he first gave to detectives. Gone was his claim that he was driving to a friend's house. Gone was his claim that he suffered a flat tire. Jassen now said that he was changing the oil in his garage at the time of the murder. When I presented him with the original story, he not only failed to recognize it as his own; he adamantly denied ever making such a statement. Jassen couldn't remember (or repeat) his original lie. The more I talked to him, the more he exposed the fact that the original story was a piece of fiction. Once he knew he had been caught in a lie, his alibi and confidence began to crumble.

Jassen was ultimately convicted of first-degree murder. The jury was convinced that the original notes from the detective were authentic and well preserved. They were convinced that they contained an accurate description of Jassen's statement from 1988. They were also convinced that Jassen's current statement was untrue.

It's important to examine the Gospels with a similar concern about their honesty and accuracy *over time*. Has the story of Jesus changed over the years? Was the truth about Jesus altered?

OPEN THE CASE FILE
(5 MINUTES – CONSIDER AND ANSWER AS MANY QUESTIONS AS POSSIBLE)

Think about the last time someone lied to you. Set aside the emotional aspects of the event and focus on the "anatomy" of the lie. Who lied to you, and what was the nature of the lie?

_____

_____

Why do you think the lie was initially successful (or unsuccessful)?

_____

_____

_____

How did you discover the claim was false? Did the person offering the lie do or say something to give themselves away?

_____

_____

_____

Liars have a difficult time being consistent with their lies over time. This "truth about lies" can help us evaluate the gospel authors.

VIEW THE VIDEO TESTIMONY
(10 MINUTES – TAKE NOTES)

Understanding why "change over time" is so critical

_____

_____

_____

Examining the concept: the "chain of custody"

_____

_____

_____

Applying the "chain of custody" concept to the Gospels

_____

_____

_____

Reexamining the claims of skeptics related to variations in the manuscripts

_____

_____

_____

Conducting a "thought experiment" with the claims of skeptics

_____

_____

_____

CONDUCT A GROUP INVESTIGATION
(25 MINUTES – INVESTIGATE THE ISSUES AND ANSWER THE QUESTIONS)

Detectives quickly learn the importance of documenting and tracking key pieces of evidence. If the evidence isn't carefully handled, a number of questions will plague the case as it is presented to a jury. Was a particular piece of evidence truly discovered at the scene? How do we know it was actually there? How do we know that an officer didn't "plant" it there? These kinds of questions can be avoided if we respect and establish the "chain of custody." Imagine, for example, that we are examining the validity of a shirt button that is being offered as a piece of evidence. The chain of custody (from the crime scene to the courtroom) might be depicted in the following way (*Cold-Case Christianity*, p. 122):

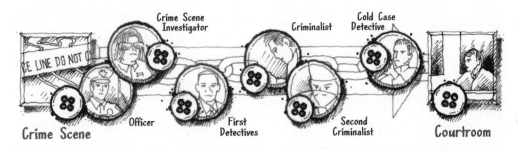

Each of these officers, detectives, and experts are links in the "chain of custody." Now let's investigate a similar "chain of custody" for the New Testament (from the life of Jesus—the "crime scene"—to a church council where the canon of Scripture was discussed—"the courtroom"). Work together as a group to review your video notes and fill in the names of each link in the following diagram:

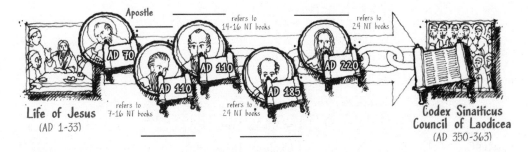

 Now, work as a group to make a list of the attributes of Jesus you think are essential to the Christian faith. Think about those truths that define the nature of Jesus and are required for Christianity to be true. List as many as you can think of on the following lines:

_____

_____

_____

_____

_____

_____

_____

_____

 Now, examine the following truths about Jesus described by just one of John's students: Ignatius. This "link" in the "chain of custody" described Jesus in the following way in his letters to local congregations. Read this description aloud:

1. The Prophets predicted and waited for Jesus.
2. Jesus was in the line of King David.
3. He was (and is) the "Only Begotten Son" of God.
4. He was conceived by the Holy Spirit.
5. A star announced His birth.
6. He came forth from God the Father.
7. He was born of the Virgin Mary.
8. He was baptized by John the Baptist.
9. He was the "perfect" man.
10. He manifested the will and knowledge of God the Father.
11. He taught and had a "ministry" on earth.
12. He was the source of wisdom and taught many commandments.
13. He spoke the words of God.
14. Ointment was poured on Jesus's head.
15. He was unjustly treated and condemned by men.
16. He suffered and was crucified.

17. He died on the cross.

18. Jesus sacrificed Himself for us as an offering to God the Father.

19. This all took place under the government of Pontius Pilate.

20. Herod the Tetrarch was King.

21. Jesus was resurrected.

22. He had a physical resurrection body.

23. He appeared to Peter and the others after the resurrection.

24. He encouraged the disciples to touch Him after the resurrection.

25. He ate with the disciples after the resurrection.

26. The disciples were convinced by the resurrection appearances.

27. The disciples were fearless after seeing the risen Christ.

28. Jesus returned to God the Father.

29. Jesus now lives in us.

30. We live forever as a result of our faith in Christ.

31. He has the power to transform us.

32. Jesus is the manifestation of God the Father.

33. He is united to God the Father.

34. He is our only Master and the "Son of God."

35. He is the "Door," the "Bread of Life," and the "Eternal Word."

36. He is our High Priest.

37. Jesus is "Lord."

38. Jesus is "God."

39. He is "Our Savior" and the way to "true life."

40. His sacrifice "glorifies" us.

41. Faith in Christ's work on the cross saves us.

42. This salvation and forgiveness are gifts of grace from God.

43. Jesus loves the church.

44. We (as the church) celebrate the Lord's Supper in Jesus's honor.

Compare this comprehensive early description of Jesus to your own (in the prior section). Cross out those attributes included in Ignatius's that you also described in your list. His list is likely much longer and more comprehensive than yours. How many more attributes of Jesus are described by Ignatius? How does Ignatius's long description of Jesus help make the case that the story of Jesus wasn't changed over time?

_____

_____

_____

John's gospel isn't the only New Testament document for which we can chart a "chain of custody." Here are the diagrams for the work of the apostle Peter (as represented in the gospel of Mark) and the work of the apostle Paul:

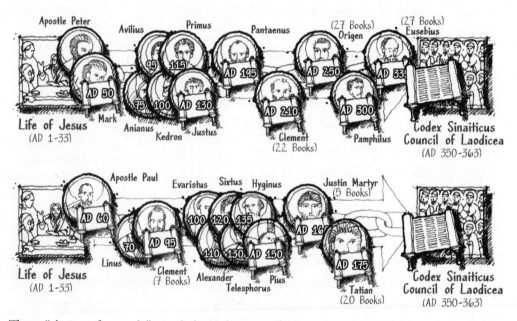

These "chains of custody" can help us have confidence that the major attributes of Jesus were described early and never changed over time. But how do we know if the other gospel details (not specifically mentioned by the students of the apostles) are accurate? One way

to be certain in this regard is to study the meticulous
way followers of Jesus handled the early manuscripts:

THE METICULOUS MASORETES

The Masoretes established comprehensive procedures to protect the text against changes:

Assign the following passages to members of
the group to read aloud: 2 Timothy 3:16–17,
1 Thessalonians 2:13, and 2 Peter 1:20–21.
How do the biblical authors describe the
Scriptures?

_____

_____

_____

_____

When an obvious error was noted in the text, it was identified and labeled, and a correction was placed in the margin.

When a word was considered textually, grammatically, or exegetically questionable, dots were placed above the word.

Detailed statistics were kept as a means of guarding against error. Leviticus 8:8, for example, was identified as the middle verse of the Torah. In Leviticus 10:16, the word "darash" was identified as the middle word in the Torah, and the "waw" located in the Hebrew word in Leviticus 11:42 was identified as the middle *letter* of the Torah.

Given this description, how might
you expect them to handle and copy
the earliest manuscripts of the New
Testament?

_____

_____

_____

_____

Statistics were also placed at the end of each book, including the total number of verses, words, and letters. By assembling statistics such as these, each book could be measured mathematically to see if there was any copyist error.

It's difficult to know with complete certainty the exact
method in which the first-century Christian scribes copied and cared for their sacred texts,
but we do know that they worked within a religious tradition that spanned hundreds of
years, both before and after the first century. The Masoretic tradition, for example, gives us
a glimpse into the obsessive care that Jewish scribes historically took with their sacred texts.

Think about the "thought experiment" described in the video. How does this description help us to have confidence in the gospel narrative even if there was a very high level of variation between copies?

_____

_____

_____

_____

TAKE A PERSONAL ASSESSMENT
(5 MINUTES – EXAMINE YOUR OWN SITUATION AND ANSWER THE QUESTIONS)

After describing the New Testament "chain of custody" to others, a friend of mine voiced a concern: "Why should we trust these early Church Fathers as credible links in the chain, when many of them disagreed about doctrinal issues, like whether baptism is required for salvation?" Has this concern come to mind as you've examined the role early church leaders played in the "chain of custody"? How might you respond to this concern?

_____

_____

_____

Imagine the following questions asked of a witness in a trial:
Question 1: "What did the suspect *say*?"
Question 2: "What do you think the suspect *meant* by what he said?"
Why do you think the first question is allowed in a criminal trial, but the second question is typically disallowed?

_____

_____

_____

Witnesses are allowed to describe what they hear a suspect *say*, but not allowed to interpret what they think a suspect might have been *thinking* (this is described as "speculation"). How can this principle help us to accept what Ignatius and Polycarp report John *saying*, while resisting any of their comments about how they interpret John's claims *theologically*?

_____

_____

_____

FORM A STRATEGIC PLAN
(5 MINUTES – EXAMINE YOUR CALENDAR AND CREATE AN ACTION PLAN)

The early Church Fathers (especially those in the first hundred years) played a significant evidential role in determining whether the truth about Jesus has been delivered to us accurately. But most of us are largely unfamiliar with these important church leaders. The more you know about them, the better prepared you will be to use them to make the case for Christianity. This week, commit to reading one of the Church Fathers described in this session. Polycarp is one choice. His letter to the Philippian church is available online. A simple search on the internet will provide several reliable sources to read this document (such as www.newadvent.org and www.earlychristianwritings.com).

Pick a Church Father you would like to read: _____

Find a website for this Church Father: _____

Select a document from this Church Father:

_____

After reading the document, what did you learn about Jesus?

_____

_____

_____

_____

MAKE A CLOSING STATEMENT
(1 MINUTE – CONTEMPLATE AND PRAY)

Jesus affirmed the timeless truth that "Man shall not live on bread alone, but on every word that comes from the mouth of God" (Matt. 4:4). The writer of Hebrews also assured us that "God wanted to make the unchanging nature of his purpose very clear to the heirs of what was promised, he confirmed it with an oath. God did this so that, by two unchangeable things in which it is impossible for God to lie, we who have fled to take hold of the hope set before us may be greatly encouraged. We have this hope as an anchor for the soul, firm and secure" (Heb. 6:17–19). God's unchanging nature has been captured on the pages of the New Testament, and these documents have been faithfully delivered to us without change.

Dear Lord, thank You for powerfully communicating the truth in Your Word. Thank You also for powerfully protecting the New Testament over many centuries of careful transmission. Help us to communicate the claims of Christianity to others as we make the case for the reliability of the Bible. Most importantly, give us the strength and clarity to tell others the most important truth they will ever hear: the offer of salvation through Your Son, Jesus Christ. May Your Holy Spirit guide our thoughts and words as we engage the people in our lives with the truth. In Jesus's name we pray, amen.

CONDUCT A SECONDARY INVESTIGATION
(READ ON YOUR OWN FOR BETTER UNDERSTANDING)

This session is more fully articulated in *Cold-Case Christianity* chapter 8: "Respect the 'Chain of Custody'" and chapter 13: "Were They Accurate?" While reading these two chapters, focus on some of the objections skeptics might offer (as described on pages 234–38) by taking notes:

Ignatius, Polycarp, and Clement Didn't Quote Scripture Precisely

_____

_____

_____

_____

_____

There Are Many Copyist Insertions That Are Obvious Corruptions

_____

_____

_____

_____

_____

There Are Many Biblical Narratives That Differ from One Another

_____

_____

_____

_____

_____

WERE THEY BIASED?

Everyone has a motive. We tend to think of criminals when we hear the word, but jurors are also encouraged to consider motive when examining and evaluating eyewitnesses who have testified in a trial. Jurors are told that they must think about whether or not a witness was "influenced by a factor such as bias or prejudice, a personal relationship with someone involved in the case, or a personal interest in how the case is decided." There are two factors at work in a question like this: bias and motive. Were the disciples lying about the resurrection, as Bart Ehrman claims? Were their claims based on religious expectation or bias? If so, what was it that they were hoping to gain from this elaborate lie? If the apostles wanted Jesus to be God, an elaborate lie wouldn't actually accomplish this, at least for the apostles. Lies might fool those who weren't there, but they wouldn't fool those who knew better. What did the disciples hope to gain if their stories were false? Let's study the issue of motive and finish our journey with an examination of Christian eyewitness bias.

In all my years working homicides, I've come to discover that only three broad motives lie at the heart of any murder. As it turns out, these three motives are also the same driving forces behind any kind of misbehavior; the reasons why we sometimes think what we shouldn't think, say what we shouldn't say, or do what we shouldn't do:

Financial Greed

This is often the driving force behind the crimes that I investigate. Some murders, for example, are the result of a botched robbery. Other murders are committed simply because they gave the suspect a financial advantage.

As an example, I once worked a homicide that was committed by a husband who didn't want his wife to receive a portion of his retirement.

Sexual or Relational Desire

I've also investigated a number of murders that were sexually (or relationally) motivated. Some victims of sexual assault are murdered by their attacker so they can't testify later. Some murders are committed simply because a jealous boyfriend couldn't bear to see his girlfriend dating another man.

Pursuit of Power

Finally, some people commit murders because a position of power or authority was jeopardized. It might be a rivalry between two people who are trying to get the same promotion. Others have killed simply because the victim dishonored or "disrespected" them in front of a group of peers.

Sex, money, and power are the motives for all the crimes that are investigated by detectives. In fact, these three motives are also behind all lesser sins as well, including lying. In this final session, we'll investigate the nature of motive and determine if the writers of the Gospels were too biased to report the history of Jesus truthfully.

OPEN THE CASE FILE
(5 MINUTES – CONSIDER AND ANSWER AS MANY QUESTIONS AS POSSIBLE)

Most of us are familiar with public scandals involving entertainers, politicians, and even religious leaders. Think about the events of the past year; can you name two or three public figures who were involved in scandals of one nature or another? Describe them here and add how you heard about the events with which they were involved:

Scandal: **How You Heard About It:**

_____   _____

_____   _____

_____   _____

_____   _____

_____   _____

_____   _____

_____   _____

 Now analyze which of the three motivations (personal biases, desire, or driving interests) might have been the underlying cause of the scandalous activity:

Scandal: **What Motivated It:**

_____   _____

_____   _____

_____   _____

_____   _____

_____   _____

_____   _____

_____   _____

How might these people have protected themselves from these temptations?

_____

_____

_____

VIEW THE VIDEO TESTIMONY
(10 MINUTES - TAKE NOTES)

Understanding why bias (motive) matters

_____

_____

_____

Repeating the three reasons why anyone does anything they shouldn't do

_____

_____

_____

Examining the motives of the gospel authors

_____

_____

_____

Reviewing how the disciples died

_____

_____

_____

Answering the objection: "I can't trust it if it was written by a Christian"

_____

_____

_____

Making a decision, given the evidence

_____

_____

_____

CONDUCT A GROUP INVESTIGATION
(25 MINUTES – INVESTIGATE THE ISSUES AND ANSWER THE QUESTIONS)

Did the alleged eyewitnesses of Jesus's life and ministry have an ulterior motive when writing the Gospels? Do we have any good reason to believe that the apostles were driven to lie by one of the three motives we have described? Let's examine the lives of the disciples through the lens of each motivation:

The Apostles Were Not Driven by Financial Gain

 Have a member of the group read Luke 18:28. What does Peter say to Jesus that might reveal something about the lifestyle of the disciples?

_____

_____

 Now read 1 Corinthians 4:11–12. What does Paul say about his financial situation?

_____

_____

 Read 2 Corinthians 6:9–10. What does Paul say about the financial condition of *all* the apostles?

_____

_____

Read Acts 20:33. What does Luke say about the attitude of Paul?

_____

_____

Given everything we know about the apostles and authors of the Gospels, how reasonable is it that they were driven by financial gain? How would you articulate this to others?

_____

_____

_____

The Apostles Were Not Driven by Sex or Relationship

 Have a member of the group read Matthew 8:14. What member of Peter's family did Jesus see in Peter's house? What does this tell us about Peter's marital situation?

_____

_____

 Now read 1 Corinthians 9:5. What does Paul say about the right of the apostles to bring their wives with them into the mission field? What does this say about the marital status of many of the apostles?

_____

_____

 Read 1 Timothy 3:2. What does Paul tell Timothy about the marital status of those who wanted to be leaders in the church?

_____

_____

Given everything we know about the twelve apostles, their marital status, and commitment to sexual propriety, how reasonable is it that they were driven by sex or relationship? How would you articulate this to others?

_____

_____

_____

THE COMMITMENT OF THE APOSTLES

The Early Church Fathers also suggested that all of the apostles were married, with the possible exception of the youngest apostle, John. Clement of Alexandria wrote that Paul, although married, did not take his wife with him when testifying as an apostle:

"The only reason why he did not take her about with him was that it would have been an inconvenience for his ministry.... [The apostles], in accordance with their particular ministry, devoted themselves to preaching without any distraction, and took their wives with them not as women with whom they had marriage relations, but as sisters, that they might be their fellow-ministers in dealing with housewives" (Clement's *Stromata*, bk. 3, ch. 5).

The Apostles Were Not Driven by the Pursuit of Power

Work as a group to list four or five attributes of "power" or authority:

_____

_____

_____

_____

_____

Have a member of the group read 2 Corinthians 11:24–28. What does Paul say he endured as someone who proclaimed the gospel? How many of the attributes you listed in the prior question appear to be possessed by Paul in this description of his life?

_____

_____

_____

Read aloud the following passage from Tacitus, the ancient Roman senator and historian (taken from his *Annals*, 15:44). This excerpt demonstrates the hostility that early Christians faced for making the claims they made. Following a great

THE MARTYRDOM TRADITIONS OF THE APOSTLES

Andrew was crucified in Patras, Greece.

Bartholomew (aka Nathanael) was flayed to death with a whip in Armenia.

James the Just was thrown from the Temple and then beaten to death in Jerusalem.

James the Greater was beheaded in Jerusalem.

John died in exile at the prison mines on the island of Patmos.

Luke was hanged in Greece.

Mark was dragged by horse until he died in Alexandria, Egypt.

Matthew was killed by a sword in Ethiopia.

Matthias was stoned and then beheaded in Jerusalem.

Peter was crucified upside down in Rome.

Philip was crucified in Phrygia.

Thomas was stabbed to death with a spear in India.

fire in Rome, Emperor Nero reportedly blamed the Christians living there: "Consequently, to get rid of the report, Nero fastened the guilt and inflicted the most exquisite tortures on a class hated for their abominations, called Christians by the populace. Christus, from whom the name had its origin, suffered the extreme penalty during the reign of Tiberius at the hands of one of our procurators, Pontius Pilatus, and a most mischievous superstition, thus checked for the moment, again broke out not only in Judaea, the first source of the evil, but even in Rome, where all things hideous and shameful from every part of the world find their centre and become popular.

"Accordingly, an arrest was first made of all who pleaded guilty; then, upon their information, an immense multitude was convicted, not so much of the crime of firing the city, as of hatred against mankind. Mockery of every sort was added to their deaths. Covered with the skins of beasts, they were torn by dogs and perished, or were nailed to torture-stakes, or were doomed to the flames and burnt, to serve as a nightly illumination, when daylight had expired."

What does this report tell us about how Christians were treated?

_____

_____

Given everything we know about the way the twelve apostles were disrespected and the way the early Christians were abused, how reasonable is it that they were driven by the pursuit of power? How would you now articulate this to others?

_____

_____

TAKE A PERSONAL ASSESSMENT
(4 MINUTES – EXAMINE YOUR OWN SITUATION AND ANSWER THE QUESTIONS)

Now that we've reached the last session of our study, let's summarize the cumulative case for the reliability of the Gospels (*Cold-Case Christianity*, p. 256):

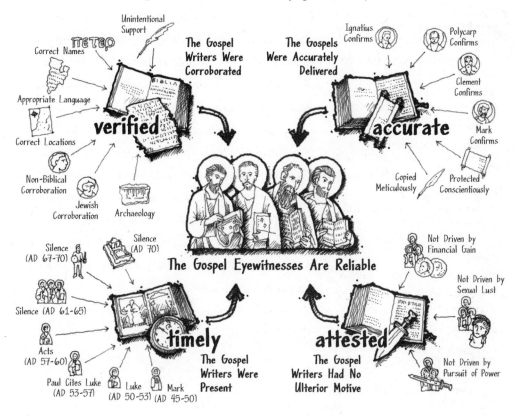

The evidence for the reliability of the Gospels has been grouped into four overarching characteristics of reliable eyewitness testimony. In our study, we've covered the majority of this evidence, but many of the additional details illustrated here can be further researched in *Cold-Case Christianity*.

Prior to doing this study, where did your concerns or doubts lie about the case for Christianity (either your personal areas of doubt or your areas of insecurity related to sharing the truth with others)?

_____

_____

_____

 Looking at the large body of evidence depicted in this diagram, how confident are you now that the case for Christianity is strong? What are the challenges to presenting a cumulative case like this to skeptics or nonbelievers?

_____

_____

_____

 Are you at all intimidated by the volume of evidence depicted in the diagram? What single category of evidence do you think you are least prepared to share with others? Why do you think this is an area where you need to improve?

_____

_____

_____

 **FORM A STRATEGIC PLAN**
(5 MINUTES – EXAMINE YOUR CALENDAR AND CREATE AN ACTION PLAN)

The surest way to improve in anything in life is to be *intentional*. If you're ready to take another step as a Christian, if you're ready to become the Christian "case maker" God has designed you to be, let this study be the catalyst for your growth and development. Don't view the time you've put into these eight sessions as an end unto itself, but rather as the beginning of a new way to approach your walk as a Christian. After you've identified the one category you'd like to study further, take the initiative to improve your knowledge:

 Identify the category of evidence you'd like to study further:

_____

 Visit the Case Files Expert Witness section of *Cold-Case Christianity* (page 265) to identify resources in this particular category for further study. List the resources you'd like to use to increase your knowledge:

_____

_____

_____

 Commit to taking the time and making the effort to become a better case maker. Select a date for completion of this study: _____

 ## MAKE A CLOSING STATEMENT
(1 MINUTE – CONTEMPLATE AND PRAY)

Not everyone is a gifted evangelist. Even Paul said that God gave "*some* as apostles, and *some* as prophets, and *some* as evangelists, and *some* as pastors and teachers, for the equipping of the saints" (Eph. 4:11–12). That means that some of us *aren't* gifted in the areas Paul described. But according to Peter, *all* of us need to "be prepared to give an answer to everyone who asks [us] to give the reason for the hope that [we] have" (1 Peter 3:15). We are called to be good Christian case makers.

 Dear Lord, thank You for creating each of us for a purpose. Help us to understand our duty and our calling as Christians. Help us to devote time in the future to study and learn, to grow and develop. Please remind us daily that

this preparation is intended for Your glory so that others may come to know You. Provide us with opportunities in the coming days to share what we've learned with others, and may Your Spirit bring to our recollection everything that You've taught us in this study. Help us to live a life that brings You glory. In Jesus's name we pray, amen.

CONDUCT A SECONDARY INVESTIGATION
(READ ON YOUR OWN FOR BETTER UNDERSTANDING)

To better understand the issues raised in this final session, read *Cold-Case Christianity* chapter 14: "Were They Biased?" While the evidence demonstrates the apostles were without bias, some skeptics continue to argue the authors of the Gospels were untrustworthy. In your additional reading, focus on the objections of skeptics (cited on pages 247–51) as you take notes:

The Gospels Were Written by Christians

_____

_____

_____

_____

_____

_____

The Death Narratives of the Apostles Were Written by Christians

_____

_____

_____

_____

_____

At David C Cook, we equip the local church around
the corner and around the globe to make disciples.
Come see how we are working together—go to
www.davidccook.org. Thank you!

transforming lives together